United States Presidents

Lyndon B. Johnson

Series Consultant:
Don M. Coerver, professor of history
Texas Christian University, Fort Worth, Texas

Michael A. Schuman

Enslow Publishers, Inc.

40 Industrial Road   PO Box 38
Box 398   Aldershot
Berkeley Heights, NJ 07922 Hants GU12 6BP
USA   UK

http://www.enslow.com

To Dick Garratt, a good friend and my
own personal clipping service.

Library of Congress Cataloging-in-Publication Data

Schuman, Michael.
    Lyndon B. Johnson / Michael A. Schuman.
      p. cm. — (United States presidents)
    Includes bibliographical references (p. 116) and index.
    Summary: Discusses the life and career of the thirty-sixth
president, whose term was filled with controversy over the civil
rights movement and the war in Vietnam.
    ISBN 0-89490-938-X
    1. Johnson, Lyndon B. (Lyndon Baines), 1908–1973—Juvenile
literature. 2. Presidents—United States—Biography—Juvenile
literature. 3. United States—Politics and government—1963–1969—
Juvenile literature. [1. Johnson, Lyndon B. (Lyndon Baines),
1908–1973. 2. Presidents.] I. Title. II. Series.
E847.S38   1998
973.923'092—DC21   97-43693
                                 CIP
                                 AC

Illustration Credits: Cecil Stoughton, LBJ Library Collection,
p. 60; Frank Wolfe, LBJ Library Collection, pp. 89, 104; Johnson
Family Photo, LBJ Library Collection, pp. 15, 16; LBJ Library
Collection, pp. 35, 62, 102, 103; Mike Geissinger, LBJ Library
Collection, p. 97; National Park Service, pp. 12, 14, 18, 101; Yoichi
R. Okamoto, LBJ Library Collection, pp. 57, 65, 69, 79, 85, 91, 94.

Source Document Credits: LBJ Library Collection, pp. 9, 24,
33, 45, 63, 71, 82, 93, 96.

Cover Illustration: Yoichi R. Okamoto, LBJ Library Collection

Contents

Acknowledgments

Special thanks go to Lyndon Johnson's former press secretaries George Reedy and George Christian, who allowed me to interrupt their schedules for personal interviews, and to E. Philip Scott, Linda Hanson, and Claudia Anderson at the LBJ Library for their professional assistance in helping me make this the best book possible.

1

A LONG
TIME COMING

P resident Lyndon Johnson took pen in hand on the evening of July 2, 1964. In the glory of the East Room of the White House, Johnson signed a bill into law.

United States presidents sign new laws routinely. Yet the law being signed on this day was not routine.

Surrounding the president were dozens of important statesmen. There were also members of the clergy, union officials, and civil rights workers. Perhaps the most famous was Martin Luther King, Jr.

They all watched as Johnson signed the Civil Rights Act of 1964. It had been a long time coming.

The roots of the Civil Rights Act dated back over one hundred years. In 1863, during the Civil War, President Abraham Lincoln issued the Emancipation

Proclamation. It declared that all slaves in the Confederate, or southern, states were to be free.

The Civil War ended in 1865. That year the Thirteenth Amendment to the Constitution was passed. That amendment formally abolished slavery in the United States.

Yet for almost a century African Americans were not completely free. In nearly all of the southern United States, segregation (separation of the races) was the law. In some cases, African Americans could not ride the same buses or trains as white persons. When they could, they had to sit in designated areas with other African Americans. They could not use the same public rest rooms or drinking fountains as whites. They could not stay at the same hotels or eat in the same restaurants. The hotels, restaurants, and rest rooms for African Americans were often filthy and run-down.

These segregation laws were based on the belief that African Americans were inferior to whites. That view is called "white supremacy."

Lyndon Johnson grew up in Texas, a southern state. Segregation was rife throughout Texas. As a teacher and legislator, Johnson had always felt uncomfortable with racist laws. Yet he knew they would not be easy to change. Segregation and white supremacy had been a way of life in the South for a long, long time. People's attitudes do not change overnight.

When Johnson became a senator, he helped arrange a compromise civil rights bill in 1957. It passed, in great part because of Johnson's work. Yet those who supported civil rights did not like the bill. They complained it was weak and gave African Americans few real rights. Yet Johnson knew a stronger bill would never be supported by southern legislators and could not pass at that time.

A newer civil rights bill had first been proposed by President John F. Kennedy. But Kennedy was assassinated in November 1963, before Congress could vote on it. There was doubt whether Kennedy would ever have gotten enough support to pass the bill.

George Christian was one of Johnson's press secretaries. He said, "Johnson believed in the power of government to do good things. There was a need for action in the area of civil rights, and he was willing to do it. It's been demonstrated since the Civil War that without government intervention some things don't change, especially concerning civil rights."[1]

Johnson refused to take no for an answer on the question of civil rights. In 1964 he declared in a commanding tone, "This bill is going to pass if it takes us all summer. And this bill is going to be signed and enacted into law, because justice and morality demand it."[2]

It would not be an easy victory. Southern senators and congresspeople knew they would have to face angry citizens at home if they voted for the bill.

In addition, many northern Republicans disliked the bill. Generally, Republicans do not support the federal government making laws that could be made instead by states or cities. They believe it is better for people to have local control over important issues.

So Johnson had to be a salesman as well as a statesman. He bargained with southern Democrats and northern Republicans. Some wanted federal money to help their home districts. Perhaps they might use that money to build a dam or a bridge. Johnson told them he could help them get their bridge or dam if they would vote with him on civil rights.

At other times he was forceful. In a private phone conversation he said to a senator, "Now you're either for civil rights or you're not. You're either the party of Lincoln or you ain't. By God, put up or shut up."[3] (When talking to people in private, Johnson often used language he felt they were comfortable with. He would never have used the word *ain't* when speaking to the general public.)

His bargaining technique proved to be somewhat successful. A few southern legislators did agree to vote for the civil rights bill. The bill passed the House of Representatives.

However, some southern senators still wanted to kill it. They tried many ways to do so. At one point they tried something called a filibuster. A filibuster is a deliberate nonstop speech delivered while a bill is being debated before Congress. Enemies of the bill planned to speak so long that the Senate would not have enough time to vote on it.

The bill wound up being debated for seventy-five

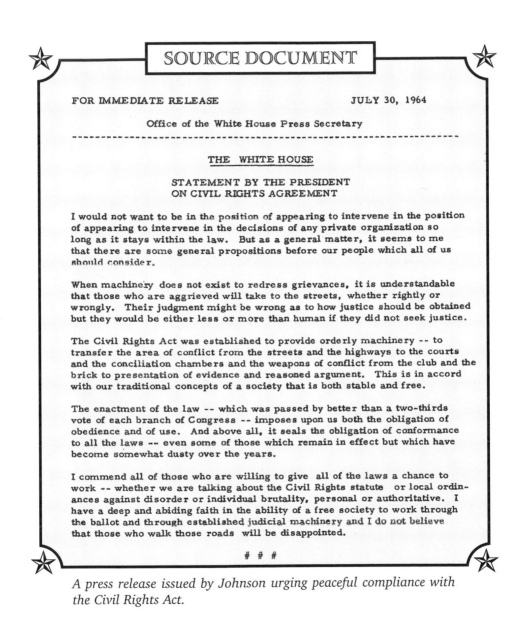

SOURCE DOCUMENT

FOR IMMEDIATE RELEASE   JULY 30, 1964

Office of the White House Press Secretary

THE WHITE HOUSE

STATEMENT BY THE PRESIDENT
ON CIVIL RIGHTS AGREEMENT

I would not want to be in the position of appearing to intervene in the position of appearing to intervene in the decisions of any private organization so long as it stays within the law. But as a general matter, it seems to me that there are some general propositions before our people which all of us should consider.

When machinery does not exist to redress grievances, it is understandable that those who are aggrieved will take to the streets, whether rightly or wrongly. Their judgment might be wrong as to how justice should be obtained but they would be either less or more than human if they did not seek justice.

The Civil Rights Act was established to provide orderly machinery -- to transfer the area of conflict from the streets and the highways to the courts and the conciliation chambers and the weapons of conflict from the club and the brick to presentation of evidence and reasoned argument. This is in accord with our traditional concepts of a society that is both stable and free.

The enactment of the law -- which was passed by better than a two-thirds vote of each branch of Congress -- imposes upon us both the obligation of obedience and of use. And above all, it seals the obligation of conformance to all the laws -- even some of those which remain in effect but which have become somewhat dusty over the years.

I commend all of those who are willing to give all of the laws a chance to work -- whether we are talking about the Civil Rights statute or local ordinances against disorder or individual brutality, personal or authoritative. I have a deep and abiding faith in the ability of a free society to work through the ballot and through established judicial machinery and I do not believe that those who walk those roads will be disappointed.

# # #

A press release issued by Johnson urging peaceful compliance with the Civil Rights Act.

days until a special vote finally called for an end to the debate. Sixty-seven votes were needed for the bill to pass. It passed by a margin of 73 to 27.[4]

The new law made several forms of discrimination illegal. For example, it was now against the law to not hire or not promote a person because of his or her race, religion, gender, or national origin. Also, no person could be stopped from entering a public building such as a restaurant, hotel, or theater for the same reasons. In addition, no school or program that received federal money could legally discriminate.

As he signed the law, Johnson said, "This is a proud triumph. Let us close the springs of racial poison."[5]

It was one of his finest hours.

2

"SUCH A FRIENDLY BABY"

L yndon Baines Johnson was a true Texan. His paternal grandfather and great-uncle had made their livings as real cowboys in the 1800s. They drove cattle from Texas to Kansas along a famous route called the Chisholm Trail.

Lyndon's mother's ancestors had fought at the Battle of San Jacinto in 1836. In Texas that battle is as famous as Gettysburg is to the rest of the United States. As a result of the battle, Texas gained independence from Mexico.

Lyndon was born on August 27, 1908, in Stonewall, Texas. It was not far from the spot his ancestors had settled. He was the first child of Rebekah Baines and Sam Ealy Johnson, Jr.

For a long time the baby had no name. His parents

simply could not decide on one. For three months they simply called him "Baby."[1] Finally one morning Sam asked Rebekah to make breakfast. Rebekah told him, "No, Sam, I am not cooking breakfast until this baby is named."[2]

Sam suggested names of relatives and friends, all of which Rebekah turned down. Finally, he suggested "Linden," in honor of a family friend named W. C. Linden. Rebekah agreed so long as the name could be spelled in a more creative way. Sam said that would be fine. In respect to Rebekah's family, baby Lyndon was given the middle name of Baines.

Lyndon Johnson grew up in a Texas that was much

This replica in the Lyndon B. Johnson National Historical Park is designed to look just like the home where Johnson was born on August 27, 1908.

different from that of his grandfather. The days of long cattle drives were over.

However, the Texas of Lyndon's boyhood was also much different from present-day Texas. Today, Texas has huge modern cities such as Dallas, Fort Worth, Houston, San Antonio, and Austin.

When Lyndon Johnson was a boy, he lived in small towns. Telephones and cars were new, and hardly anyone had either. In fact, there were no paved roads in the towns where Lyndon lived. All the streets were dirt. After a good rain, they became mud.

None of the homes nearby had electricity or running water. The Johnsons used a two-door outhouse as a bathroom. Rebekah Johnson did the family laundry outdoors with a tub and a washboard.

Lyndon's father tried to make a living as a farmer. He also served in the state senate in the Texas capital of Austin. Even with those two jobs he had to struggle to earn enough money to support his family.

Rebekah Baines Johnson was an unusual woman for her day. She had a college education and was trained as a journalist. At the time, it was expected that women would give up their careers to stay home and take care of their children. Rebekah did what was expected.

Lyndon was an outgoing baby. When he was less than a year old, his parents took him to a neighborhood picnic. Lyndon smiled at the guests. He tried to climb out of his father's arms and into theirs. After watching Lyndon's actions, a neighbor said, "Sam, you've got a

This fireplace in the east bedroom of Johnson's birthplace was a source of warmth during the winter in Texas.

politician there. I've never before seen such a friendly baby. He's a chip off the old block. I can just see him running for office twenty-odd years from now."[3]

Lyndon was especially close to his mother. Rebekah gave him special attention. She taught him to read the alphabet before he was two. When he was two, his mother gave birth to a baby girl, also named Rebekah. Two years later, she had another baby. This was a girl named Josefa.

Even with two baby sisters, Lyndon stayed close to his mother. He said that his first real memory was of his mother crying by the water pump in front of the farmhouse. Lyndon was about two or three. His father was working late and was away from home. Johnson recalled, "It was dark; we didn't have lights then, and I could hold the lamp while she pumped the water. I remember she was crying, and she said she was frightened. I told her I'd take care of her."[4]

Within walking distance of Lyndon's birthplace is the

Lyndon Johnson's mother, Rebekah Johnson.

Pedernales River. He once said, "I first remember walking along the banks of the Pedernales when I was a boy of about four or five . . . from the little home where I was born down the river up to my grandfather's house where he would always give me peppermint stick candy or a big red apple."[5]

As a boy, Lyndon liked to roam away from home. He would wander in the tall Texas fields by himself or with his pet collie, Rover. His mother often worried that he would get bitten by a rattlesnake or fall into the river.

Rebekah had Lyndon memorize poetry by age three and spell words by four. When he was four, his mother started him in public school. Most children did not begin until they were five or six. The school was just one room, and children from grades one through eight learned from one teacher.

The tiny size of the school concerned Sam and

Johnson at six months old.

Rebekah Johnson. When Lyndon was five, they moved fourteen miles to the nearest town, Johnson City. It had been named for Lyndon's great-uncle who had settled it in the 1800s. They hoped Lyndon would get a better education in a bigger school.

The Johnsons' new home had only six rooms but was one of the nicest in town. Like most homes in Johnson City, it had no plumbing or electricity. When Lyndon was six, his mother had another baby. It was a boy named Sam Houston Johnson. Two years later, Rebekah had her last child, a girl named Lucia.

Sam Ealy Johnson tried to earn more money by taking on more jobs. In addition to farming, he tried buying and selling cattle. He also dabbled in real estate. Sometimes he made a lot of money. Most of the time he did not. Out of frustration, he began to drink alcohol.[6] Sometimes, when he was drunk, he would beat his children.[7] However, when he was sober he was very kind to his family.

Although Rebekah Johnson loved her oldest son, at times she was unusually hard on him. If Lyndon brought home a poor report card, she would ignore him for days. One time he quit both violin and dance lessons. Johnson later said, "For days after I quit those lessons she walked around the house pretending I was dead. And then to make it worse, I had to watch her being especially warm and nice to my father and sisters."[8]

As he grew older, Lyndon became known as a neighborhood troublemaker. A boyhood friend named Joe

Johnson's six-room boyhood home in Johnson City, Texas.

Payne remembered that Lyndon often got into fights. Sometimes he stole peaches from his grandfather's tree. Lyndon liked to rebel against authority figures. He often disobeyed his parents.

In school, he did not do homework and he skipped classes. When he was twelve and in the eighth grade, Lyndon was absent fifty days of the school year. He was also late for thirty of the one hundred thirty days he was present.[9]

Once his teacher told him he would have to miss recess because he had not done his homework for several days. He walked outdoors toward recess anyway. When passing the classroom window he spit at the teacher. She punished him by placing him inside an ice shack. Lyndon screamed loudly and pushed at the door with the force of a moose. When the teacher opened the door to let him out, Johnson fell forward and bloodied his nose.

In spite of his behavior, Lyndon managed to earn pretty good grades. He did well in the subjects he liked. In other classes, he used his charm to get by. Sometimes Lyndon convinced girls in his class to do his homework for him. If he was called on and did not have an answer, he would squirm his way out of the situation by cracking a joke or distracting his teacher.

Although he disobeyed his parents, Lyndon loved them.

Sometimes his father took him to Austin when the state legislature was in session. Johnson said, "I loved going with my father to the legislature. I would sit in the gallery for hours watching all the activity on the floor . . . The only thing I loved more was going with him on the trail during his campaigns for reelection."[10]

In 1924, Lyndon finished eleventh grade. It was the final grade of his high school. Since he started school at such a young age, he graduated when he was fifteen. He was tall for his age. At graduation, he stood at six feet.

There were five other students in his graduating class. The class prophecy said Lyndon would some day become the governor of Texas.

He could have gone on to college. But Lyndon still had a rebellious streak. He felt his dream life was out West. He left for California in July 1924 with four other young men. It took them ten days to make a car trip that one could easily make in three days today.

Once reaching California, they went their separate ways. Lyndon moved in with a cousin named Tom Martin in San Bernardino, about sixty miles east of Los Angeles. Martin was a lawyer, and he hired Lyndon as a law clerk. Lyndon hoped Martin would train him to become a lawyer.

After working with Martin for a while, Lyndon discovered a shocking surprise. His cousin was practicing law without a license, clearly breaking the law. Lyndon eventually returned home, after spending a little over a year in California.

Still, he did not want to go to college. He took a job with a road construction crew in Texas. Most of the time he worked with a dirt scraper pulled by mules. The job paid little and the labor was backbreaking. He worked outdoors in all conditions. These included pouring rain, the scorching summer sun, and the biting cold of winter.

Finally Johnson had enough. A friend named Stella Glidden remembered, "It was one bitterly cold day. He came in from the highway and he said, 'I'm ready to go to college now.'"[11]

In 1927, Johnson left for the town of San Marcos, about fifty miles away. Southwest Texas State Teachers College (SWTTC), where Johnson hoped to become a student, was there. He was nineteen years old.

3

"I NEVER HAD
A CHANCE, BUT
YOU DO"

In order to take classes at Southwest Texas State Teachers College (SWTTC), Johnson had to pay for them. The problem was that he had hardly any money. He could not borrow any from his father. Sam Ealy Johnson had troubles of his own. He was broke and deeply in debt.

To earn money, Lyndon took a boring and exhausting job. He joined a campus clean-up squad at the college. He moved rocks, picked weeds, and emptied garbage. Yet even the money he earned from his job was not enough to pay for classes. So Johnson spoke with a local bank president named Percy T. Brigham. Brigham had once worked for Johnson's grandfather. Johnson was able to convince Brigham to loan him money for college.

There was one other big problem. Johnson had to prove he was a good enough student to be admitted into the college. Because his high school had only eleven grades, it was not accredited. That means it did not meet certain standards and was not recognized as a quality school.

To be enrolled in SWTTC, Johnson entered what was called a subcollege. In subcollege, he had to write essays and pass tests. If he did, he would earn the right to become a student.

Johnson was worried. He said, "I thought sure it was back to the road gang for me."[1]

He studied like he had never studied before. His essays were very well received. One essay he wrote was good enough to be published in the college newspaper. The subject was how society treats nonconformists. Nonconformists are people who choose not to live the same way most others do. In school, a nonconformist might wear clothes other students consider out of style or outlandish. They might have ideas that students or teachers consider either radical or old-fashioned.

The subject of plane geometry almost killed Johnson's chances of getting into college. Rebekah Johnson came to San Marcos to help her son. Johnson said, "My mother sat up all night . . . trying to get me to memorize enough plane geometry to get me admitted to college."[2]

Johnson took the plane geometry test and received a 70 out of 100 points. That was the lowest possible passing grade. But it was good enough for admittance to SWTTC. The spring semester started on March 21, 1927. Johnson enrolled and was officially a college freshman.

At first his grades were only fair. He received a D in debate, two Cs, and two Bs. In addition, he was low on money. Johnson tried to get by on two meals a day but was hungry much of the time. He thought seriously of dropping out and returning to California.

Johnson wrote to a friend named Ben Crider. Crider was one of the young men Johnson had traveled with to California. At the time Johnson wrote the letter, Crider was working in a cement plant. Lyndon's mother knew her son was discouraged and asked Crider to help persuade Lyndon to stay in school.

Ben wrote back and told Johnson he could get him a job at the cement plant. However, he added that it was miserable work. Crider also did a special favor for Johnson. He loaned him eighty-one dollars. It was Crider's entire savings.[3] Crider wrote, "I never had a chance, but you do. I'm sending you every dollar I've got. Now you stay in school."[4]

Johnson accepted that money and paid his debts. Then he took a second job as a school janitor.

The struggling student decided to get a two-year teaching degree as quickly as possible. He did not take summers off. He discovered he had to work even more hours to earn enough college money, so he took other menial jobs. These included stuffing envelopes and

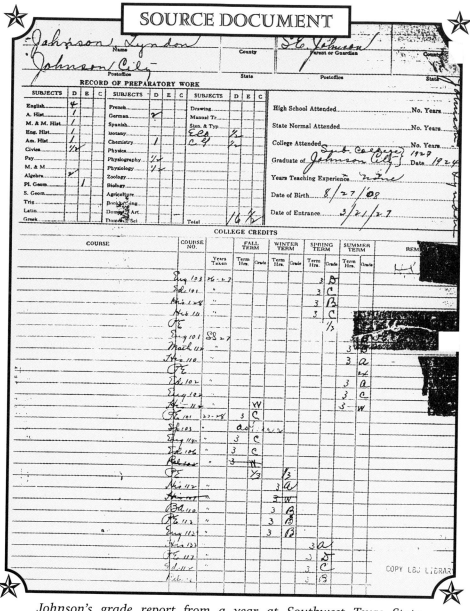

Johnson's grade report from a year at Southwest Texas State Teachers College.

selling socks door-to-door. A professor said, "He was such a salesman, you couldn't resist him."[5]

Since there were many more women than men at SWTTC, Johnson had little trouble getting dates. There was one special young woman named Carol Davis. Johnson said she was

> . . . very beautiful, tall and blond with dark blue eyes. Her skin was pale and very soft. She was very clever and everyone admired her. I fell in love with her the first moment we met. . . . I still remember the summer evenings we spent together, lying next to the river in a waist-high mass of weeds, talking about our future. I had never been happier. After a while we began to talk about marriage.[6]

Johnson took courses through six straight terms and graduated at the end of summer 1928. His first job was teaching grade school in a little Texas town called Cotulla. It was just sixty miles from the Mexican border. Most of his students were Mexican Americans living in poverty.

Johnson later said, "I was determined to help those poor little kids. I saw hunger in their eyes and pain in their bodies. . . . I was determined to give them what they needed to make it in this world, to help finish their education."[7]

He was known as a strict but excellent teacher. At the time, it was legal and common for teachers to spank children who misbehaved. One boy named Danny Garcia later said,

> The three grades the president taught were combined. There were about thirty of us. He used to leave us in

> class on our honor. One day I got up in front of the room
> and was clowning around. The president came tiptoeing
> back in. He took me by the hand and led me into his
> office. I thought I was going to get a lecture, but that
> wasn't it. He turned me over his knee and whacked me
> a dozen times on the backside.[8]

Although he was tough, Johnson went out of his way to help his students. Garcia also said, "This may sound strange but a lot of us felt he was too good for us. We wanted to take advantage of his being here. It was like a blessing from the clear sky."[9]

A girl named Dorothy Nichols remembered, "There was one boy—I don't remember his name—who couldn't pass the English test to get into the high school, so Lyndon took him home and he and his mother tutored him. I understand he did pass the test."[10]

At the time Johnson was teaching in Cotulla, his girlfriend, Carol Davis, had a teaching job just thirty-five miles away in a town called Pearsall. Johnson visited her on weekends. However, by now they were drifting apart. Her parents did not approve of the romance. They thought Johnson's family was beneath hers. In time Carol and Lyndon also learned they had very different interests. She loved opera and hated politics. He was bored with opera and thrived on politics. They soon broke up.

After a year of teaching, Johnson went back to college. He wanted to get a full bachelor's degree. Johnson reentered SWTTC in September 1929. By August 1930 he had earned the degree. Johnson had completed in one year the amount of work most students normally took two years to finish.

Just before he graduated college, Johnson gave a speech at a rally for a local politician named Pat Neff. Neff was a former governor running for the state railroad commission. Johnson had a personal interest in Neff's election. Neff had helped Johnson's father get a job as a bus inspector. If Neff lost, Sam Ealy Johnson might be out of work again.

Johnson's speech was a big hit. One man who was impressed with it was named Welly Hopkins. Hopkins was running in a Democratic primary election for state senate. He asked the tall, thin, twenty-one-year-old Johnson to be his campaign manager. As part of the job, Johnson organized rallies and gave speeches in four counties in south-central Texas. Hopkins won with ease.

Johnson then took a job teaching in Pearsall, the same town his ex-girlfriend Carol Davis had taught in. Soon a job opened up in Houston, the biggest city in Texas. For a young Texan who wanted to move up in the world, the big city was the place to be.

In the fall of 1930, Johnson became a speech and debate teacher at Sam Houston High School in Houston. Although he had done poorly in a debate course as a college freshman, Johnson enjoyed the art of debating. He promised the principal that he would lead the school's debate team to the city championship. The principal found that hard to believe. Sam Houston High had never achieved that honor.

Those who joined Johnson's debate team were in for hard work. The teacher asked that his students give up their afternoons for debate practice. He also asked them to give up their evenings to do research. However, the time turned out to be well spent. The team easily won the city championships. They also won the district championships. Then they went on to take part in the state championships. Boys and girls competed on separate teams. The girls lost early while the boys lasted until the final round. However, they lost in that round on a tight vote: three to two against them.[11]

Even though his students did not win the big prize, Johnson had turned them into local celebrities. The Houston newspapers published articles about the team. Johnson also convinced *The Houston Post* newspaper to award a cash prize to the team members.

Johnson became very well regarded at the school. In fact, he was one of the few teachers to receive a raise for the next year. In the 1930s the country was suffering through the Great Depression. It was one of the most difficult economic periods the nation has ever been through. Jobs were hard to come by, and millions of Americans were out of work. For those who had jobs, raises were generally out of the question.

However, Johnson stayed in his teaching position for only a few months. A man named Richard Kleberg was running for Congress. Kleberg's campaign manager was Roy Miller. Johnson's old friend and former employer Welly Hopkins had recommended to Miller that he try to get the support of both Sam Ealy and Lyndon Johnson.

As soon as Kleberg won, Hopkins suggested to the new congressperson that he hire the young schoolteacher to be his secretary. The title of the job is misleading. Today Johnson would be called a congressional aide. His job was to help manage Kleberg's office.

Johnson took a leave of absence from his teaching job and headed to Washington, D.C. A new career was waiting.

4

LANDSLIDE LYNDON?

Lyndon Johnson packed up and moved to Washington. He began working for Congressman Richard Kleberg in December 1931. Johnson soon learned that Kleberg did not take his job seriously. Kleberg was from a wealthy family and never had to work hard for a living. Time he should have devoted to work was spent playing golf or traveling for fun. Before long, Johnson was running Kleberg's entire office.

Johnson lured two of the students from his high school debate team to Washington to help out. He turned out to be as tough a boss as he was a teacher. One student, Luther E. Jones, later said, "Lyndon Johnson was a hard man to work for because he insisted on perfection. Everything had to be just right, and it had to be the way *he* wanted it."[1]

But he was just as hard on himself. Johnson worked long, intense hours. It did not matter whether he was in his Washington office or on a business trip.

On one such trip in August 1934 he was in Austin, Texas. Through a mutual friend there he met a twenty-one-year-old woman named Claudia Alta Taylor. However, nobody called her by her given name. She was known by the nickname Lady Bird. When she was a baby, a nurse had looked at her and said, "Why, she's as purty as a ladybird!"[2] The nickname stuck for life.

Like Lyndon, Lady Bird grew up in a small Texas town. Unlike Lyndon, she grew up in a wealthy home. Her father was a successful farmer and store owner. In some ways, Lady Bird was similar to Lyndon's mother. She had graduated college and studied journalism.

Lyndon asked Lady Bird if she would care to meet for breakfast the next morning. She liked him, but felt he came on strong. She recalled, "He had lots of wavy black hair, quite handsome. I was very impressed, and a little bit inclined to run because I thought I had met up with something intense."[3]

For whatever reason, Lady Bird did not run. She and Lyndon enjoyed breakfast together the next morning. Then the couple went for a drive. Before the day was over, he asked her to marry him. They had not even known each other a full day. She later said she thought he was joking. He was not.

She would not answer right away. Within days Johnson took her to meet his parents. On the way back to Washington, Johnson stopped to meet her father, Thomas Taylor. He was impressed and told Lady Bird, "Daughter, you've been bringing home a lot of boys. This time you brought a man."[4]

Three months later they were married. After a honeymoon in Mexico, the couple settled in a one-bedroom apartment in Washington. Johnson continued to work for Kleberg. As he did, he got to know important people in the world of politics.

Then a special opportunity arose. President Franklin Roosevelt had been fighting the Great Depression by forming government agencies. The purpose of the agencies was to create jobs. People took jobs constructing bridges, building schools, or crafting works of art. The difference was they were working for the government rather than for a private company.

Having the government employ so many people had never been done before and was a radical idea for its time. Roosevelt's philosophy of government programs was called the New Deal. Johnson strongly supported these programs. He believed in guaranteed jobs for poor and powerless people like his own family.

One New Deal agency was called the National Youth Administration (NYA). Its goal was to help young people either stay in school or get training for jobs.

Roosevelt hired Johnson in 1935 to direct the NYA in Texas. Johnson was twenty-seven years old. He was not much older than many of the young people he was hired

No. 104133

THE STATE OF TEXAS
COUNTY OF BEXAR

To any Regularly Licensed or Ordained Minister of the Gospel, Jewish Rabbi,
Judge of the District Court, Judge of the County Court or Justice of the Peace:

You, or either of you, are hereby authorized to solemnize or join in the

HOLY UNION OF MATRIMONY

Lyndon B Johnson and *Bird Taylor*

in accordance with the Laws of this State and that you make due return of this, your authority,
to my office, in sixty days from date hereof, certifying how you have executed the same.

Given under my hand and the seal of the County Court of

Bexar County, this 17th

day of November 1934

Jno W Huntress Jr.
County Clerk, Bexar County

By Joe C Froboese Deputy

The foregoing License executed by me, joining the within named parties in the
HOLY UNION OF MATRIMONY

this the Seventeenth day of November 1934

Two Witnesses Sign here: *Cecille Harrison* / *Thayer Hinselberg*

Official Performing Ceremony: *Arthur K McGinty* / *Pastor Godman*

Returned the 24 day of Nov 1934   A true copy of the original

Recorded this the 24 day of Nov 1934

By Joe C Froboese Deputy   Jno W Huntress Jr. Clerk

The Texas marriage license of Lyndon B. Johnson and Lady Bird Taylor. One can see both their signatures in the middle of the page.

to help. He was also the youngest such director in the nation.[5]

In the first year, Johnson helped eighteen thousand young people return to high school.[6] At the same time he helped another twelve thousand find jobs.[7]

Although Johnson enjoyed success with the NYA, two years later he decided to take a gamble. The congressperson who represented the region of Texas that included Johnson City suddenly died. A special election was to be held to fill the vacancy. Johnson decided to run for Congress.

In the presidential election of 1936, more than 85 percent of Texas voters cast ballots for Roosevelt.[8] Johnson was well known in the state for his support of the president. That helped him win the 1937 congressional election. Lyndon Johnson was only twenty-nine years old and a member of Congress.

Soon afterward, Roosevelt visited Galveston, Texas, while on a cruise of the Gulf of Mexico. He invited Johnson to visit him there. Johnson took advantage of the situation by getting to know Roosevelt better. The young member of Congress made small talk with the president. He asked Roosevelt about his family and whether he had had any luck fishing while on his trip. He knew Roosevelt had a special interest in the Navy, so Johnson made sure to discuss different types of warships with him.

When Roosevelt returned to Washington he told an aide, "I've just met the most remarkable young man.

Johnson (far left) and his four siblings on Christmas 1936, only months before he would become a congressman.

Now I like this boy, and you're going to help him with anything you can."[9]

Johnson used his friendship with the president to help bring rural Texas into the modern world. Many people in Texas did not have the comforts and conveniences we take for granted today. One of these was electricity.

An officer of the Pedernales Electric Co-op, which provided electricity to south-central Texas, was named E. "Babe" Smith. Smith discussed life before electricity. He said, "It was a rather primitive life—no running water and no refrigeration. Every meal had to be started from scratch. They used to say a man was a gentleman who provided his wife with a sharp axe to cut the wood with."[10]

Johnson helped get millions of dollars' worth of modern buildings and facilities built in Texas. These included houses, libraries, roads, and dams. Water power provided by the dams helped bring electricity to much of his state.

Smith remembered, "My daughter—she was about nine years old—she just couldn't believe how the house had lit up. She said, 'Mama, the house is on fire.'"[11]

Johnson was as proud as a new parent. He later wrote, "Of all the things I've ever done, nothing has ever given me as much satisfaction as bringing power to the hill country of Texas."[12]

A popular representative, Johnson was reelected in both 1938 and 1940. By 1941 he was ready for something new. One of Texas's senators had died before completing his term. As was the case in 1937, a special election would be held to fill the vacant seat. Johnson decided to run for the Senate.

Texas is a huge state and Johnson's name was not well known outside his district. A poll released on April 21, 1941, showed him with only 5 percent support.[13] The election was to be held June 28. He had his work cut out for him.

However, Johnson was not an average campaigner. He worked as hard as a Texas mule. He labored from dawn to dusk, visiting all corners of the massive state.

He sought out farmers at work in their fields. He chatted with owners of small town stores. A poll released on election day showed Johnson with 31.2 percent of the vote. He was leading every other candidate. In just two months Johnson's support had increased from 5 to over 30 percent.[14]

Johnson's toughest opponent was the sitting governor, who had the colorful name of W. Lee "Pappy" O'Daniel. O'Daniel was much more conservative than Johnson.

When nearly all the votes were counted, *The Houston Post* trumpeted a front-page headline that read, "JOHNSON WITH 5152 LEAD, APPEARS ELECTED."[15]

Today the media use computers to project election results. Sometimes a winner can be known even before all the polls close. But the computer was just a dream in 1941. In isolated towns and villages, it often took days for votes to be reported and counted.

It was also common for illegal votes to be cast in much of Texas. Sometimes names of dead people were placed on lists of registered voters. One person might vote several times, using these names. This practice is called stuffing the ballot box.

When *The Houston Post* headline appeared, O'Daniel's supporters knew exactly how many votes he needed to win. And they found illegal ways to get them. When the last ballots were counted, O'Daniel had won by 1,311 votes.[16] Lyndon Johnson had learned a tough lesson about Texas politics.

Johnson went back to serving in Congress. However, the biggest news of 1941 was yet to happen. On December 7, Japan bombed the American naval base at Pearl Harbor, Hawaii. In 1941, Japan was a military dictatorship. For several years Japan had been invading and occupying its neighboring countries. In Europe, dictatorships in Germany and Italy were doing the same. The world was a scary and dangerous place.

After the attack on Pearl Harbor, the United States declared war on Japan. Within days, Germany and Italy announced they would side with Japan against the United States. The United States was now deeply involved in a major bloody and monstrous war. This was to be known as World War II.

Although he was thirty-three years old, Johnson volunteered for active duty in the U.S. Navy. Sent to the South Pacific, he was stationed in Australia and New Guinea. One day, he was flying as a passenger officially observing a bombing mission. His plane was attacked and nearly shot down. He was awarded a special honor called the Silver Star. Its purpose is to honor bravery in action.

Some critics later said that Johnson did not earn his Silver Star. Other men on the same plane received no medals. Some believed Johnson received his medal only because he was in Congress.

Roosevelt felt congresspeople were of more value to their country at home than at war. On July 1, 1942, the president ordered all members of Congress to return home. On July 16, Johnson was back at his old job in Washington.

The poverty of Lyndon's boyhood was never far from his mind. He wanted to avoid ever falling back into that condition, so he and Lady Bird decided to invest some of her money in a private business. They bought a radio station in Austin.

Soon there was other news in the Johnson family. Lyndon and Lady Bird had been trying to have children for years. Over that period Lady Bird had had three miscarriages. Then in March 1944, Lady Bird gave birth to a daughter whom they named Lynda Bird Johnson.

World War II ended in 1945. By that time, the oil industry had become the biggest business in Texas. In general, people who own or work for oil companies have conservative views. Johnson knew that. In order to keep the support of his fellow Texans, he began publicly to steer away from his liberal positions.

Being a southern state, Texas was also very conservative about race relations. Johnson came out against civil rights issues. Harry Truman, now president, was pushing for civil rights reform. Johnson announced, "The civil rights program is a farce and a sham—an effort to set up a police state in the guise of liberty."[17]

On the other hand, Johnson did continue to support those liberal issues that helped the people of his state. These included government programs to build roads and houses, and to bring electricity to even more remote areas of Texas.

In 1947, Lady Bird gave birth to another daughter. She was named Lucy Baines. That was not the only major change in the Johnsons' lives. Lyndon was running once again for the Senate. An election would take place in 1948.

Johnson's main problem was winning the Democratic party nomination. The Democrats were much stronger than the Republicans in Texas. It was fairly certain that the Democratic nominee would beat the Republican opponent in the general election.

As in 1941, Johnson's major competitor was the sitting governor. This time it was Coke Stevenson. Like Pappy O'Daniel, he was more conservative than Johnson.

Johnson added a gimmick to this campaign. He traveled across the state in a helicopter. Many people had never seen one. Some went to Johnson campaign stops just to watch the funny-looking mechanical bird.

Six days after the election, the last votes came in. These included 202 votes from the small south Texas town of Alice. Of that total, 200 were for Johnson and two were for Stevenson. With these votes, the final total was 494,191 for Johnson and 494,104 for Stevenson. Of almost a million votes cast, Johnson won by a tiny margin of 87 votes.[18]

Some observers said all the votes in Alice were written in the same handwriting. Others said all the names were in alphabetical order. Did people stuff the ballot box in favor of Johnson? If so, did Johnson know about it? Or was it done by regional Johnson supporters without his knowledge? It did not matter. Johnson was the winner of the Democratic primary.

His opponents mocked him. An election victory by a huge margin is called a "landslide." To make fun of Johnson's narrow victory, Johnson's political enemies called him "Landslide Lyndon."

Johnson went on to beat his Republican opponent easily in the general election.

As Senator Johnson, he voiced some conservative views. This was especially true concerning civil rights. In speeches he stressed that he hated racism. However, he said the answer was not laws from the federal government. He insisted that civil rights laws should instead be passed by individual states. This policy is called "states' rights."

Just two years after taking office in the Senate, Johnson was awarded an important post. The party whip is responsible for keeping order in his or her party. The whip also makes sure as many party members as possible attend meetings and vote. Since Johnson was known for his ambition and hard work, his fellow Democrats named him Democratic party whip in 1951.

Though the Johnsons lived in faraway Washington, their hearts were always in Texas. In 1951 they bought a large, rambling house on a ranch in Stonewall, not far from where Lyndon was born. It had a swimming pool and a big yard, perfect for a Texas-sized barbecue.

Johnson later said about the ranch house,

> I first came to this house as a very young boy. . . . My
> uncle and aunt lived here. They would always ask all the
> in-laws to come here and spend their Christmas. . . . And
> I'd spend three months' vacation from school riding with
> [my uncle] and looking after the cattle. I kept coming
> back to this house. I guess I must have had a yearning to
> someday own it.[19]

Away from politics, the Johnsons complemented
their radio station by buying a television station. It, too,
was located in Austin. Since he owned both a radio and
a television station, Johnson excused himself from
voting on issues in the Senate that had to do with
television or radio. Voting on such issues would have
been a "conflict of interest." That means that Johnson
might have had something personal to gain from his
vote. A person in that situation might not vote honestly
and objectively.

One issue that Johnson took a definite stand on was
communism. In the 1950s, the United States was one of
two superpowers in the world. The other was the Union
of Soviet Socialist Republics (USSR), also known as the
Soviet Union. The USSR consisted of Russia and fourteen other republics that are now independent nations.
During World War II, the Soviet Union fought on the
same side as the United States. However, once the war
was over, the two superpowers became enemies.

The USSR practiced communism whereas the
United States practices capitalism. In capitalism,
businesses are privately owned. In pure communism,
there is no private business. Manufacturing and services
are owned by the community. Communism in the Soviet

Union was different. All businesses and property were owned directly by the government. There was only one official political party—the Communist party. People who disagreed with the Communist party were often sent to jail or forced from their homes.

Many Americans were afraid that the USSR wanted to force communism on the United States. Some believed the Soviets might attack the United States. World War II was fresh in Americans' minds. It seemed to many that the Soviet Union was trying to control other countries, just as Germany and Japan had done a few years earlier.

Meanwhile, Soviet leaders told their citizens that the United States wanted to force its ways of life on the Soviet people. Because no actual fighting ever took place, this dispute between the USSR and the United States was called the "Cold War." The Cold War would not end soon.

In Congress Johnson urged the United States to spend more money on defense. That way there would be enough military might to counter any attack made by the USSR.

In 1954 Johnson was reelected to the Senate. He won by a nearly three-to-one ratio over his conservative opponent.[20] The Democrats also gained control of the Senate.

Johnson was becoming well known as a man of action. He was famous for his ability to convince people. An aide named Liz Carpenter said, "I don't think anybody has ever topped him at trying to be persuasive. He would grab you by the lapel and just say, 'We wanna get this done!'"[21]

His aggressive way of trying to convince people to support his views eventually became known as the "Johnson treatment."

Johnson was named the Senate majority leader in 1955. That means he was the leader of his fellow Democratic senators, then the majority party in the Senate. Johnson was the youngest majority leader in history. He was only forty-six years old.[22]

Not all was good news in 1955. That summer the senator suffered a serious heart attack. He was a heavy cigarette smoker and lived on a diet of fatty junk food. His long work hours were stressful.

For a while it looked as if he might not survive. It took six months for Johnson to recover fully. He quit smoking and began eating sensibly. He toyed with the idea of running for president in 1956, but rejected it. Then, in 1957, he was put to the strongest test of his career as a senator.

A major civil rights bill was being voted on in the Senate. Johnson was stuck in the middle. Privately, he supported rights for African Americans. However, he did not want to anger the Texans he represented. He worked hard to get both sides to compromise on many issues and helped work out the Civil Rights Act of 1957.

One important part of the act stated that violating someone's right to vote because of his or her race is

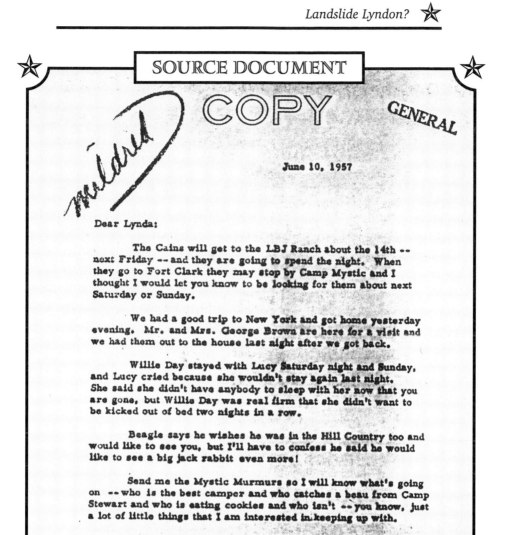

SOURCE DOCUMENT

COPY

GENERAL

June 10, 1957

Dear Lynda:

The Cains will get to the LBJ Ranch about the 14th -- next Friday -- and they are going to spend the night. When they go to Fort Clark they may stop by Camp Mystic and I thought I would let you know to be looking for them about next Saturday or Sunday.

We had a good trip to New York and got home yesterday evening. Mr. and Mrs. George Brown are here for a visit and we had them out to the house last night after we got back.

Willie Day stayed with Lucy Saturday night and Sunday, and Lucy cried because she wouldn't stay again last night. She said she didn't have anybody to sleep with her now that you are gone, but Willie Day was real firm that she didn't want to be kicked out of bed two nights in a row.

Beagle says he wishes he was in the Hill Country too and would like to see you, but I'll have to confess he said he would like to see a big jack rabbit even more!

Send me the Mystic Murmurs so I will know what's going on -- who is the best camper and who catches a beau from Camp Stewart and who is eating cookies and who isn't -- you know, just a lot of little things that I am interested in keeping up with.

A heart full of love to my beautiful daughter.

Your Daddy

Lyndon B. Johnson

Miss Lynda Bird Johnson
Camp Mystic
Hunt, Texas

LBJ M

Senator Johnson writes his daughter Lynda Bird, hoping to keep her from being homesick at summer camp.

against the law. Those accused of doing so would be given a trial in a state court. Many African Americans were unhappy with that part of the act. They felt any trial should be held in federal court, because it was unlikely at the time that a jury in a southern state would ever rule in favor of an African American.

Still, the law was viewed as a victory for civil rights. In the eyes of the nation, Lyndon Johnson proved he could separate himself from the southern senators who always voted against civil rights.

Johnson said,

> Maybe I voted wrong on some civil rights bills in the past, but I'm learning all the time. I got all I could on civil rights in 1957. Next year I'll get a little more, and the year after that I'll get a little more. The difference between me and some of my northern friends is that I believe you can't force these things on the South overnight.[23]

5

INTO THE OVAL OFFICE

L yndon Johnson had one hobby in his life: politics. One of his friends and aides was Texas politician John Connolly. Connolly recalled how he and Senator Johnson attended football games together. They rarely discussed the action taking place on the field. Johnson only wanted to talk about the goings-on in the United States capitol.

Although Senate majority leader was a powerful position, Johnson had his mind on the other big white building in Washington: the White House. Johnson wanted to be president of the United States. First he had to win the Democratic party nomination.

Johnson had the most experience of all the Democrats running for president in 1960. Two of his stronger Democratic opponents were Minnesota senator Hubert Humphrey and Massachusetts senator John F. Kennedy. Both Humphrey and Kennedy were seen as liberals, especially in terms of civil rights. Because Johnson had defended states' rights on racial issues, he was viewed as a moderate.

However, there had not been a southern president since before the Civil War. (Woodrow Wilson was born in Virginia and raised in the deep South. However, he was governor of New Jersey when he was elected president in 1912.)

Perhaps no candidate from a southern state could have been elected president in 1960. After all, legal segregation was a way of life in the South. Many residents in the rest of the United States found the practice hateful and would never vote for anyone who lived where segregation flourished.

Kennedy won the majority of the state Democratic primary elections and the nomination. He was young (forty-three), handsome, and articulate. The retiring president was Dwight D. Eisenhower, who was sixty-nine years old. Kennedy represented a new generation and new ideas.

At the Democratic National Convention in the summer of 1960, Kennedy had to choose a vice-presidential running mate. Presidential candidates often select running mates who are different from themselves. That way the two candidates can appeal to a wide range of voters.

Kennedy was a liberal Democrat from a northern

state. He was also Roman Catholic. There had never been a Catholic president. In 1928, a Catholic Democrat named Al Smith had run for president. Smith was a target of much anti-Catholic prejudice. Some of it was truly vicious.

Texan Lyndon Johnson was a moderate and a Protestant. He would appeal to residents of the South who did not relate to a liberal, Catholic northerner. He was a natural choice.

Yet the vice-president has few real powers. Johnson was used to being in command. Still, Johnson accepted Kennedy's offer to run for vice-president. Many wondered why he would take the job.

Jack Valenti was a close aide to Johnson. Valenti said he thought Lady Bird had a lot to do with the decision. Valenti stated, "I think Mrs. Johnson wanted him to. I think that she felt like the vice-presidential post would be a less onerous [demanding] post. . . . The heart attack in 1955 I suspect really preyed on Mrs. Johnson's mind. You must recall that that was little more than four and a half years after that heart attack."[1]

Valenti added that he believed Johnson never thought he would become president. Valenti said, "I know he often said that no man born in the South would ever be nominated for President in his lifetime. . . . I think there's no question about it, that he expected to live out eight years of his vice-presidency and then probably retire at the age of sixty."[2]

Kennedy won a very close election over Republican

Richard Nixon. However, Johnson was unhappy as vice-president.[3] After years of holding powerful positions, now he had to answer to someone else. To make matters worse, the president was younger than Johnson and had far less experience as a legislator.

There was also the matter of the president's education. Kennedy graduated from Harvard University, one of the most respected universities in the United States. Most of Kennedy's advisors had attended top-level colleges or universities. Johnson received his college degree from a small state school in Texas. Because of this difference, Johnson felt inferior to Kennedy and to his staff.[4]

Above all, what made Johnson most unhappy was the job itself. Kennedy tried to keep Johnson busy. He named Johnson the head of two agencies. One was the Presidential Committee on Equal Opportunity. It was a group that helped find ways to further the cause of civil rights. The other was the Space Council.

Johnson also traveled on official trips abroad. He made eleven trips in which he visited thirty-three countries.[5] That kind of world travel might sound glamorous to some. But to Lyndon Johnson, the trips only took him farther away from the excitement and action at home.

Indeed, much was taking place in the United States. In southern cities and towns, African Americans were marching in the streets to protest segregation and other unfair racial laws. Their most noted leader was Dr. Martin Luther King, Jr.

In 1962 Kennedy banned discrimination in housing owned or supported by the federal government. He then pushed for a law with even more muscle. It would outlaw segregation in all public buildings.

At the same time, the Cold War was still raging. The idea that a free country might fall to communism was frightening to many Americans. Some thought that if one nation was taken over by Communists, then all the nations in that region would topple like dominoes. That line of thinking was known as the domino theory.

The little country of Vietnam is in southeast Asia. It is about as far as any nation can be from the United States. At the time, Vietnam was divided into two countries. North Vietnam was Communist. South Vietnam was non-Communist.

North and South Vietnam were fighting a civil war. Some Americans feared that North Vietnam would overtake South Vietnam and make it a Communist country. Kennedy sent United States military advisors to aid South Vietnam in their war effort. The South Vietnamese had a rough fight ahead. They were battling both North Vietnam and some South Vietnamese, known as the Vietcong, who supported communism.

All the time Johnson was busy with his travels, he never forgot his family. His aide Liz Carpenter recalled the time Johnson made a special trip just for his daughter. She said, "The time Lynda made top grades at the University of Texas, he happened to be flying to California for a speech. And he came back through

Texas to see her and congratulate her with a big box of clothes. And I remember him just looking at her and saying, 'I love you so much.'"[6]

Johnson's job gave him time to spend with his family that he had not had before. Daughter Lynda mentioned how her father now was home for family dinners. It was a rare break from an otherwise hectic life. It was also a less stressful time. Major decisions facing the nation were temporarily out of his hands. This included the situation in Vietnam.

From the time John Kennedy took office through the fall of 1963 he greatly increased the number of United States military advisors in South Vietnam. In January 1961, there were less than one thousand advisors. By the fall of 1963, there were over sixteen thousand.[7] Still, Kennedy never sent combat troops. In fact, in September 1963, Kennedy appeared to say that the United States should play a smaller role in Vietnam.

Kennedy stated, "In the final analysis it is their war. They are the ones who have to win it or lose it. We can help them, we can give them equipment, we can send them our men out there as advisors, but they have to win it, the people of Vietnam against the Communists."[8]

What Kennedy would have done regarding Vietnam will never be known. Kennedy was assassinated on November 22, 1963, while riding in a motorcade with the Johnsons in Dallas, Texas. Without warning, Lyndon Johnson was now president of the United States.

Many people might have panicked under those

circumstances. But Johnson was in complete control. After it was confirmed that Kennedy had died, Johnson and Lady Bird were driven to a nearby Dallas airport. They then boarded the official presidential airplane known as Air Force One. With them were Kennedy's widow, Jacqueline, and the president's body.

Johnson had arranged for a judge named Sarah Hughes to be on board to administer the oath of office. No presidency is legal until the incumbent swears to abide by the oath. Hughes read it and Johnson repeated the words. His first presidential order was, "Let's get this plane airborne."[9]

Within minutes he told his staff to call the slain president's mother, Rose Kennedy. Johnson told her, "Mrs. Kennedy, I wish to God that there was something that I could say to you, and I want to tell you that we're grieving with you."

Rose Kennedy answered, "Thank you very much. That's very nice. I know you loved Jack and he loved you."[10]

Johnson landed at Andrews Air Force base just outside Washington late in the afternoon. As he stepped off the airplane, an army of newspaper and television reporters were waiting for him.

He told them, "This is a sad time for all people. We have suffered a loss that cannot be weighed. For me it is a deep personal tragedy. I know the world shares the sorrow that Mrs. Kennedy and her family bear. I will do my best. That is all I can do. I ask for your help—and

God's."[11] That was Johnson's first address as president to the people.

Back in Dallas, authorities tried to find who fired the shots that killed President Kennedy. All evidence pointed to a former Marine named Lee Harvey Oswald. Oswald worked in a building called the Texas Schoolbook Depository. The building overlooked the motorcade route. Oswald was captured in a movie theater hours after the assassination.

Oswald was never put on trial. Just two days after he was captured, he was shot to death by a Dallas night-club owner named Jack Ruby. Because Oswald was not alive to tell his story, there were many unanswered questions about Kennedy's death. On November 29, 1963, Johnson named a special commission to investi-gate the assassination. The commission chairman was Chief Justice of the United States Earl Warren. It became known as the Warren Commission.

Johnson knew which senators, congresspeople, and other government leaders he wanted on the commis-sion. He would not take no for an answer. One person he wanted was a Georgia senator and personal friend named Richard Russell.

Russell and Warren did not get along. Warren was Chief Justice of the Supreme Court that had ruled on a case called *Brown* v. *Board of Education* in 1954. The case outlawed school segregation. As a native of the deep South, Russell was a strong supporter of segregation. When Johnson told Russell he was needed on the commission, Russell replied, "I just can't sit on that commission with Chief Justice Warren. I don't like that man. I don't have any confidence in him."[12]

Johnson answered abruptly. He told Russell, "You're my man on that commission and you're going to do it. And don't tell me what you can do and what you can't. You're goddam sure going to serve. I'll tell you that."[13] Russell served on the commission.

Every January the president of the United States makes a special speech to the nation. It is called the State of the Union address. Its purpose is to inform the American citizens how things are going in the nation. Presidents often use that speech to introduce new ideas or programs.

On January 8, 1964, Johnson gave his first State of the Union address. He declared a different kind of war. It was a "War on Poverty."

Johnson later wrote,

> There were still 35 million Americans living beneath the poverty line when I became President—in an era of growing prosperity. The poor were, and are, a continual ache in the nation's heart. . . . The final decision to wage what came to be known as the War on Poverty was made over the Christmas season of 1963—just a month after I took office—at my ranch in Texas.[14]

Johnson decided he would help the nation in the same way his hero, Franklin Roosevelt, had done. He would create government programs to help people make their lives better.

Some of the programs were the following:

1. Volunteers in Service to America (VISTA), in which Americans would volunteer their time to teach and help poor and disadvantaged Americans.

2. The Job Corps, which would provide job training for disadvantaged young people (ages sixteen to twenty-one).

3. Head Start, a special teaching program for needy preschoolers.

4. The Work Study Program, which offered jobs to people so they could work while attending college. That way they could afford to pay tuition and boarding costs.

5. The Work Experience Program, which provided day care to poor parents.

Franklin Roosevelt had called his group of government programs the New Deal. Johnson called his the Great Society.

He traveled across the country trying to drum up support for the Great Society. He pleaded with those who came to hear him. In one speech he said, "Our first objective is to free thirty million Americans from the prison of poverty. Can you help us free these Americans? And if you can, let me hear your voices."[15]

The audience responded with applause and cheers. Then in July came the moment of triumph when the Civil Rights Act of 1964 was passed.

While Johnson was fighting for the War on Poverty,

the other war was going on—the undeclared one raging in Vietnam. On August 2, 1964, American military leaders outside Washington received a disturbing report. It said that an American destroyer named the *Maddox* had been fired upon at night by North Vietnamese torpedo boats. Another similar attack was reported two days later. These incidents were said to have taken place in waters off the North Vietnam coast called the Gulf of Tonkin.

That may have been why Johnson made what came to be called the Tonkin Gulf Resolution. It said in part,

The president and Jack Valenti, a close aide to Johnson, meet briefly in the White House front hall in 1964.

". . . the United States is, therefore, prepared, as the President determines, to take all necessary steps, including the use of armed force, to assist any member or protocol state of the Southeast Asia Collective Defense Treaty requesting assistance in defense of its freedom."[16]

In a nutshell, the resolution stated that the United States would fight as it wished against the Communists.

The Tonkin Gulf Resolution had to be approved by Congress. On August 7, the House of Representatives passed it 416 to 0. The same day, the Senate passed it 88 to 2.

In response to the *Maddox* incident, the United States retaliated by bombing North Vietnam.

It was never proven that an attack by North Vietnam ever took place. No sign of a ship, such as an oil slick, was found the mornings after the attacks were said to have taken place. To this day many believe no such attacks really occurred.

Others disagree. One is Robert McNamara, secretary of defense for Presidents Kennedy and Johnson. McNamara insisted the attacks did happen. He later wrote, "The evidence of the first attack is indisputable. The second attack appears probable but not certain."[17]

Only Congress can declare war. However, a Johnson aide named Clark Clifford later said that the Tonkin Gulf Resolution ". . . was about as close a declaration of war as one could get. That started us down the long road of Vietnam."[18]

6

ONE REMARKABLE YEAR

T he year 1964 was an election year. The 1964 Democratic National Convention took place in mid-August in the resort town of Atlantic City, New Jersey. Johnson was easily renominated. For his running mate he chose liberal Minnesota senator Hubert H. Humphrey.

Johnson was incredibly popular. It was less than a year since Kennedy's assassination, and most Americans wanted to continue Kennedy's programs. Johnson was supported by people in all walks of life.

One of America's greatest writers of the twentieth century, John Steinbeck, wrote,

> We have one of the best prepared, most effective Presidents in our history. . . . Lyndon Johnson loves government and loves what he is doing. When other

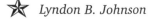

men took long weekends, arranged tours which amounted to vacations, he worked in his office doing what he liked to do. The result was and is that he can outwork anyone in government and that without strain or exhaustion.[1]

At their national convention the Republicans nominated an Arizona senator named Barry Goldwater. Goldwater was an ultraconservative who accused the Democrats of being soft on communism. He went so far as to suggest using "low-yield nuclear bombs" in Vietnam.[2]

To many, Goldwater's talk of using nuclear weapons seemed reckless. At one point he announced, "I wanted

During his 1964 campaign, Johnson visited families in the Appalachian Mountains.

to educate the American people to lose some of their fear of the word 'nuclear.' When you say 'nuclear,' all the American people see is a mushroom cloud. But for military purposes, it's just enough firepower to get the job done."[3]

Anti-Goldwater bumper stickers said, "Vote for Goldwater and Go to War."[4]

Johnson contrasted himself with Goldwater in his campaign speeches. On many occasions, he insisted he would not send combat troops to Vietnam. One time he said, "Some others are eager to enlarge the conflict. They call upon us to supply American boys to do the job that Asian boys should do. They ask us to take reckless actions, which might risk the lives of millions and engulf much of Asia."[5]

In September, the Warren Commission released the results of its investigation into President Kennedy's assassination. The commission concluded that Lee Harvey Oswald, acting alone, shot and killed President Kennedy. It also reported that Jack Ruby, acting alone, killed Oswald. At the time, the majority of Americans accepted these conclusions.

On November 4, 1964, Americans went to the polls. The results of this election were much different from the figures in 1960. It was not close. By the evening of election day, it was obvious that Johnson had won a tremendous victory. He beat Goldwater by nearly 16 million votes.[6] In the electoral college, Johnson earned 486 votes to Goldwater's 52.[7] Unlike in his 1946 Senate

Lady Bird Johnson frequently helped out during her husband's 1964 campaign.

election victory, Lyndon Johnson was now truly Landslide Lyndon.

In addition, the Democrats won overwhelming control of the House of Representatives and the Senate.

Johnson later said, "It was a night I shall never forget. Millions upon millions of people, each one marking my name on their ballot, each one wanting me as their President. . . . For the first time in all my life I truly felt loved by the American people."[8]

REPORT OF THE WARREN COMMISSION ON THE ASSASSINATION OF PRESIDENT KENNEDY

Introduction by
HARRISON E. SALISBURY
with additional material prepared by
THE NEW YORK TIMES
exclusively for this edition

McGRAW-HILL BOOK COMPANY
New York • London • Toronto

The Warren Commission's report on the assassination of President Kennedy was accepted by the American public at first. Over the years it has become a subject of controversy.

Johnson did not have much time to savor his victory. The two main problems facing the country—Vietnam and civil rights—were turning into crises.

For the most part, the United States was fighting the Vietnam War on the defensive. In January 1965, Johnson's advisors were convinced that the United States' war policies must include a more aggressive role. National Security Advisor McGeorge Bundy met with Secretary of Defense Robert McNamara. Bundy then sent a memo to the president. He wrote, "Bob [McNamara] and I believe that the worst course of action is to continue in this essentially passive role which can only lead to eventual defeat and an invitation to get out in humiliating circumstances."[9]

Johnson had much on his mind. Should the United States take a stronger role in Vietnam? Or should he keep his campaign promise to keep the United States out of the conflict and let South Vietnamese soldiers do most of the fighting?

If the United States pulled out, would America's other allies lose faith in the United States' promises to protect them? Would South Vietnam lose the war and become a Communist nation? If the domino theory turned out to be correct, would other nearby countries be taken over by Communists? Would Johnson then go down in history as the first president of the United States ever to lose a war?

There were two more questions: If Johnson was viewed as a quitter, would Congress lose respect for him as president? If so, would he be able to get Congress to pass his Great Society programs?

Then there was the other side. If the United States increased its presence in Vietnam, more American fighting men would surely die. Children would lose fathers in a war being fought in a country on the other side of the world with no direct connection to the United States.

What was Johnson to do?

Johnson later wrote, ". . . I knew we were at a turning point."[10]

His advisors gave him three choices:

1. Continue the present course, knowing it might not work.

Sitting in the Oval Office, Johnson watches three different news reports on Vietnam.

2. Bomb North Vietnam and Vietcong strongholds heavily.

3. Start a gradual bombing program.

Johnson chose the third option. In February he ordered air strikes against North Vietnam. He hoped the bombing would force North Vietnam to stop fighting and begin to consider peace talks. The series of air attacks was called Operation Rolling Thunder. Yet all Operation Rolling Thunder succeeded in doing was to make the North Vietnamese even more determined to keep fighting.

Less than a month later, Johnson ordered two battalions of Marines to protect an air force base in South Vietnam. Those were the first United States combat troops to play an active role in the war. Johnson had broken his campaign promise about not sending American boys in to fight a war that Asian boys should be fighting.

At home, African Americans were continuing to protest discrimination in large demonstrations. Although the Civil Rights Act of 1964 banned legal segregation, there were still unfair laws in effect in much of the South. Some southern politicians knew that if African Americans were allowed to vote, they might lose their elections. So they made it difficult for African Americans to vote. In several southern communities, African Americans had to pay a tax to vote. Some would not pay this illegal tax. Others simply did not have the money.

Another method of making it difficult for African Americans in the South to vote was a so-called literacy test. African Americans had to answer questions about state laws or other topics. Those who could not answer them correctly were not allowed to vote. Many white citizens could not have passed these "tests." However, they were never asked to do so.

In March 1965, Martin Luther King, Jr., tried to lead a nonviolent march from Selma, Alabama, to the state capital of Montgomery. He hoped to draw attention to these unfair voting laws. As the marchers tried to cross a bridge outside the Selma city limits, they were beaten by local police and other citizens. The day became known as Bloody Sunday.

On March 15, Johnson went on television and introduced a voting rights bill. He said, "Their cause must be our cause, too. Because it's not just Negroes but really it's all of us who must overcome the crippling legacy of bigotry and injustice. And we shall overcome."[11]

Johnson had been referring to a popular civil rights anthem called "We Shall Overcome." Also, "Negroes" was an acceptable term for African Americans then; at the time it was not a racial slur.

Johnson ordered four thousand troops into Selma to protect the marchers.[12] With the troops' protection, the march from Selma to Montgomery took place without further major incidents.

Around that same time, Johnson pushed through Congress his Great Society programs. Included were some he had already introduced in his War on Poverty. There was also the Water Quality Act to clean up water pollution. Other laws designated money for national parks and public television.

Laws to protect consumers were passed as well. One made it illegal for companies to lie about what they wrote on their products' packages. Yet another created the National Endowment for the Arts and the National Endowment for the Humanities. These help fund projects such as plays, documentary films, and museum exhibits. Most artists are not well paid and do not have the large amounts of money needed to complete such works.

Money to fund artistic works would come from the federal government. As Johnson convinced congress-people and senators to vote for his programs, it was obvious that the "Johnson treatment" was still successful.

On April 17, 1965, the president was vacationing at his Texas ranch. It was the place he went to escape the pressures of Washington. On that same day back in Washington some fifteen thousand young people gathered at the White House to protest the increased United States presence in Vietnam.[13] They demonstrated non-violently and demanded the United States withdraw its troops at once. Most were young and ultraliberal. They did not speak for the majority of Americans then.

Soon there was a problem in another foreign country. This one was closer to home.

The Dominican Republic is located on the island of Hispaniola in the Caribbean Sea. Sharing the island with the Dominican Republic is the country of Haiti.

In late April the president of the Dominican Republic was overthrown. The country's military forces took over. Also fighting to gain control of the nation were rebels thought to be Communist. There was chaos in the streets of Santo Domingo, the country's capital.

As with most countries, the United States had diplomats in Santo Domingo. There were also American tourists who happened to be on vacation there when the unrest broke out. Johnson sent forces of United States Marines to help protect the Americans in Santo

April 11, 1965—Johnson gives his friends a ride in his amphibious car in the Pedernales River. Only days later, Vietnam protesters would march on the White House.

Domingo. Many wanted to get out of the country. They were safely evacuated.

The Marines were to serve another purpose. The nearby island nation of Cuba had been taken over by Communists in 1959. The Cold War was still real. Johnson wrote, "The situation in the streets of the Dominican capital was alarming. Our Embassy reported that guns had been passed out at random—many to Communist organizers, who were putting them into the hands of their followers."[14]

The last thing Americans wanted was two Communist countries so close to home. It was up to the Marines to help prevent a Communist takeover.

Johnson announced in early May that he was sending more troops to Santo Domingo. They did their job, and by the end of May American troops started to return home. A peacekeeping force took their place.

Such was not the case in Vietnam. Johnson got the United States deeper into the war in the summer of 1965. For the six months from January 28 to July 28, 1965, United States fighting forces were increased from twenty-three thousand to one hundred seventy-five thousand troops.[15] On July 28 he announced on television to the nation that he was sending fifty thousand more troops to South Vietnam.[16] The United States was now deeply involved in the war.

Most Americans continued to support Johnson and his Vietnam policies. The Great Society was popular,

⭐ | SOURCE DOCUMENT | ⭐

PROMPTER *BEGINS*

July 28, 1965

Not long ago I received a letter from a woman in the midwest. She wrote: "Dear Mr. President, In my humble way I am writing to you about the crisis in Vietnam . . . I have . . . a son who is now in Vietnam. My husband served . . . in World War II. . . . Our country was at war, but now this time it's something I don't understand, why?"

I have tried to answer that question a dozen times and more. I have discussed it fully in Baltimore in April, in Washington in May, and in San Francisco in June. Let me now discuss it again. Why must young Americans -- born into a land exultant with hope and golden with promise -- toil and suffer and sometimes die in such a remote and distant place.

The answer, like the war itself, it not easy. But it echoes clearly from the painful lessons of half a century. Three times in my lifetime -- in two World Wars and in Korea -- Americans have gone to far lands to fight. We have learned -- at a terrible and brutal cost -- that retreat does not bring safety, or weakness, *bring* peace.

This excerpt from a press conference dated July 28, 1965, shows Johnson's intention to increase fighting forces in Vietnam.

too. On July 30, Johnson signed another law that would affect the lives of nearly every American.

The bill Johnson signed into law was called Medicare. It was an extension of Social Security. It provided health insurance for people age sixty-five and older. Included were hospital care, nursing home care, and outpatient services. Harry Truman had tried to get a national health care law passed when he was president. Truman's law would have covered not just the elderly but every American citizen. People who supported Truman believed health care was a right, not a privilege. However, Truman was unable to get his health care program passed by Congress.

Johnson's Medicare was a remnant of what Truman had hoped to create. If it did not take care of all United States citizens, at least it protected the elderly. In honor of Truman, Johnson traveled to the ex-president's home in Independence, Missouri. Johnson signed the law at the Truman Library with eighty-one-year-old Harry Truman looking on. Truman told Johnson, "You have made me a very, very happy man."[17]

To this day, all American citizens sixty-five and older are covered by Medicare.

The president's pen was busy that summer. Just over a week after he signed Medicare into law, Johnson signed another important bill.

This time the issue was civil rights. All the hard work of Martin Luther King, Jr., and others had finally paid off. On August 6, 1965, Johnson signed the Voting

Rights Act of 1965. It banned poll taxes, literacy tests, and other unfair methods of making it hard for minorities to vote.

Johnson said, "So we will move step by step—often painfully, but I think with clear vision—along the path toward American freedom."[18]

Press Secretary George Christian said that of all the bills Johnson signed into law, the most difficult to pass were those relating to civil rights. Christian noted that Johnson would not accept compromise. "Civil rights was probably his number one headache," Christian recalled. "He had to convince enough Southern Democrats and enough Republicans to get the bills passed, and there was no way he could compromise. He had to fashion something that clearly insured the right to vote, or someone would find a way around it."[19]

Within a week, all Johnson's hopes for progress between the races were jolted. The problem began in Watts, a mostly African-American neighborhood in Los Angeles. In Watts, a twenty-one-year-old African-American man was arrested for drunk driving. Local African Americans charged police brutality. That means they accused the police of physically abusing the suspect.

Watts erupted in huge riots. African Americans took to the streets. They started fires, vandalized cars, broke into stores, and stole merchandise.

The riots lasted six days, from August 11 to 16. A total of thirty-four people died. Over one thousand were injured. Property damage was great. It was estimated at over 40 million dollars.[20]

Some say Johnson had trouble understanding what brought on the riots. Others disagree. George Reedy was another press secretary who served under Johnson. Reedy explained,

> I think he [Johnson] fully understood that there was a difference between law and reality. Johnson signed laws to help blacks but there were never enough appropriations [money] to make those laws work. I argued with him all the time on this. Some poor black man might know a law was signed, but he'd look up in his building and see a window still broken, and the cold air coming in and he'd believe blacks had been taken for a ride—that whitey sold us out again.[21]

There was also a huge difference between African Americans in and outside the South. In the South, laws could change things. However, in the North and West, there had been no poll taxes or segregation laws. A different kind of segregation existed. It was caused by poverty, unemployment, and prejudice. No law could change people's attitudes. That was true in both the North and the South.

In some ways, African Americans in northern and western cities were even more angry than those in the South. For decades, prejudice and poverty forced them into the lowest-paying jobs in the most dangerous neighborhoods. African Americans outside the South were not hired in high-paying jobs because many whites considered them inferior. To these African Americans, white people in general were the enemy.

A civil rights activist named James Farmer said the following about African Americans living in northern cities: "They were not like the poor blacks and Mexican-Americans that [Johnson] had had contact with down in Texas. They were different. . . . They were angry people. They were belligerent folk. They did not see Lyndon Johnson as a friend. They saw Lyndon Johnson as a white man."[22]

From this point on, the civil rights movement would no longer consist mainly of nonviolent protests.

Roger Wilkins was an African-American member of Johnson's staff. Wilkins said, ". . . [Johnson] never understood it. . . . He did not understand that generations of heaping inferiority into our souls needed to be purged. And if you're going to put that awful stuff into people, when people begin to expel it it's not coming out pretty."[23]

The Watts riots were a clear example of this type of purging.

7

JOHNSON'S WAR

B y 1965 Johnson was in his late fifties. Yet he refused to slow down. He continued working long, exhausting hours. Often he slept as little as four hours a night.

Press Secretary George Christian recalled, "He worked around the clock. His style was to work two 'work days.' He worked in the morning and early afternoon. Then he took a nap from 3 P.M. to 4 or 4:30 and started his day over, shaving and showering and staying in his office until 11 P.M."[1]

In time, the stress caught up with him. On October 8, 1965, Johnson entered a Maryland hospital. In a two-hour operation, he had his gallbladder and a kidney stone removed. While still in a hospital bed, he went back to work on government business.

A few days later, Johnson was resting with his doctor on the hospital grounds. Reporters asked him about his surgery. Suddenly Johnson lifted up his jacket and shirt. He proudly showed them the long diagonal scar on his belly that was the result of the operation. Some Americans were shocked that a president would do something so crude.

As he went back to work, Johnson hoped he would be able to sit down and negotiate a settlement with North Vietnam. In December, the United States announced that in the spirit of the holiday season it would stop bombing North Vietnam.

On Christmas Eve, 1965, the United States suspended its bombing missions. The purpose of the truce was also to give North Vietnam a show of faith. Perhaps North Vietnam would now agree to peace talks.

Johnson pleaded, "We are ready now as we have always been to move from the battlefield to the conference table. I have stated publicly and many times again and again America's willingness to begin unconditional discussions with any government at any place at any time."[2]

Yet North Vietnam had no interest in negotiating with the United States.

Why was North Vietnam so stubborn? Were the Communists trying to take over the world? Many Americans and military leaders thought so.

The leader of Communist North Vietnam was Ho Chi Minh. Although Ho was a Communist, many now believe that his main goal was to unify Vietnam rather than spread communism. To Ho, the war was a civil war being fought between the Vietnamese of the north and those of the south. In some ways it was like the United States' own Civil War of 1861–1865.

At the time, many Americans did not understand Ho's position. Secretary of Defense Robert McNamara later wrote, "We . . . totally underestimated the nationalist aspect of Ho Chi Minh's movement. We saw him first as a Communist and only second as a Vietnamese nationalist."[3]

Why did so many intelligent leaders like Johnson and McNamara misread leader Ho Chi Minh's goals? McNamara explained that one reason was because China, Vietnam's mighty neighbor, was very hostile toward the United States and other democracies.

Another reason was Cuba. The Caribbean island was far from the Soviet Union in terms of distance. Yet Cuba was a Communist country linked with the Soviet Union. Cuba seemed to be proof that communism must be stopped before it started appearing in all parts of the world.

More and more American fighting men died as the war continued. In 1965, the total of American deaths was 1,369.[4] In the year 1966, a total of 5,008 more would be killed.[5]

As the death toll grew, so did the protests. On March 31, 1966, more than twenty thousand people marched

Johnson and Secretary of Defense Robert McNamara. The two men were responsible for much of the military buildup in Vietnam.

down Fifth Avenue in New York City to demonstrate against the war.[6]

Some young people burned their draft cards. By doing so they were saying they would not fight in Vietnam even if they were drafted. Their actions were illegal. Some went to jail. Others moved to Canada to avoid the draft.

Of course, there was one way Johnson could have won the war. It would have been easy.

The United States had ended World War II by dropping two atomic bombs on Japan. The United States had the power to do the same to North Vietnam and quickly end this war. To many Americans, it would have been the right course of action. They felt their nation was fighting with one hand tied behind its back. If the United States were to use its ultimate power, the atomic bomb, the war would quickly end.

To others, this solution was unthinkable and inhumane. About one hundred fifty thousand people died instantly in the two atomic bomb attacks on Japan. It is estimated that another fifty to sixty thousand later died as a result of wounds caused by the bombings.[7] Who knows how many innocent civilians would have died in such a similar bombing raid on North Vietnam?

Years later, Lady Bird Johnson was asked if her husband ever considered dropping an atomic bomb. She answered, "Not by his order, but there was a part of this country who wanted to do it that way and get it [the war] over with. He was scareder [sic] of that than he was of the people on the left."[8] (The term *left* refers to liberals who opposed the war. *Left wing* is often used as a term to describe people supporting liberal causes. *Right wing* refers to political conservatives.)

However, there was one victory on the foreign scene. All American troops had left the Dominican Republic. On June 1, 1966, free elections were held there. A moderate politician named Joaquin Balaguer was elected president.

Yet the return of democracy to the Dominican Republic was not on the minds of most Americans. They were too concerned with the thousands of young men dying in southeast Asia. At the same time, they were beginning to lose faith in President Johnson's honesty. Johnson told the American people that the United States was winning the war. Several times he stated that peace was at hand.

Americans questioned whether his statements were true. If so, then why was the war dragging on? Why did we need to send so many more troops? The word *credible* means believable. If you describe a person as credible it means you have faith in that person. Americans were beginning to think Johnson was not credible. There was talk of a "credibility gap" between President Johnson and the American people.

A joke was being told in Washington. The question was, "How do you know when Lyndon Johnson is telling the truth?" The answer was: When he pulls his earlobe or strokes his chin he's telling the truth. But when he starts moving his lips, that's when he's not telling the truth.[9]

Was Johnson misleading the people on purpose? There are different views. Doris Kearns Goodwin is a writer who spent a great deal of time with Johnson in the 1960s and early 1970s. She said Johnson's statements to the nation were part of the old "Johnson treatment" he had used so well back in the Senate. But what worked face-to-face with members of Congress did not work with the American public.

Goodwin explained,

> He was so used to using words as a means of persuasion . . . so used to talking to seven different people telling them seven different things so they would all come

SOURCE DOCUMENT

March 25, 1966

Dear Dale:

I understand that you are still touring the country showing off our cattle and winning prizes.

Only this time, I see where you have won a prize -- re-election as President of the Blanco County Hereford Association, and I want you to know how proud I am of you.

May I say congratulations -- and offer my most heartfelt thanks to you, Jewel, and the children for all the hours of dedication and hard work you selflessly give to the true home of the Johnson family.

With affectionate best wishes,

Sincerely,

LYNDON B. JOHNSON

Mr. Dale Malechek
Foreman
LBJ Ranch
Stonewall, Texas

Johnson says thank you to Dale Malechek, the foreman of the LBJ Ranch. Even at a time when Johnson's credibility was being questioned by many Americans, he was able to detach himself from the pressures of office to maintain personal friendships.

together to do what he wanted, that lying and persuasion were all part of the same thing for him. And I don't think he even knew the truth. I'm not sure there was truth for him. . . .

But when you're president and you make statements, and those statements are then picked up and they're put on television, you're not just talking to seven different southerners and northerners who will never speak to one another. Suddenly you get this credibility gap because people hold you to your statements.[10]

Johnson's press secretary, George Reedy, disagreed with Goodwin. Reedy noted,

There was a simple reason for the credibility gap. For a while I too was believing all the reports from Vietnam, that we were winning and all that. Then after I left the White House I ran into a man who had been one of the people who went around the villages of South Vietnam asking questions of the villagers, and he told me [about what he did].

He said his presence might make him a target of the Vietcong. To the villagers he was a menace. So the villagers would tell him what he wanted to hear just to get rid of him.[11]

Reedy explained that what Americans wanted to hear was the same thing the South Vietnamese government wanted to hear. "They wanted to hear that we were winning the war. The White House just got back radar echoes of all that Johnson was sending out. And Johnson believed what he was told."[12]

The news at home was not good, either. During the hot summer of 1966 there were more race riots in America's cities. Chicago, Cleveland, and New York City were hard hit in July that year.

There was one bright spot for the Johnson family in 1966. Luci married a young man named Patrick Nugent on August 6. (Luci had changed the spelling of her first name from "Lucy.") The ceremony took place at a Washington church. The reception was at the White House and over seven hundred people attended.[13] Lady Bird was so happy. She wrote in her diary, "By 11 the great, great day was over—happily, beautifully, to our hearts' delight—a part of the memories of this great White House."[14]

Lady Bird was an active first lady throughout her years in "this great White House." She was often traveling. Sometimes she examined firsthand how her husband's War on Poverty programs were doing. Other times she tried to boost Americans' interest in seeing their country. She loved nature and promoted America by taking rafting trips or exploring its national parks.[15]

Her greatest passion was an attempt to beautify the nation's highways and towns. She dedicated new parks and gardens and made appearances at tree plantings. Thanks to her efforts, a law called the Highway Beautification Act was passed. It limited the raising of signs on federal roads and called for improved highway planning.

Though the nation's highways might have been beautiful, by 1967 its mood was ugly. African Americans continued to vent their anger in the streets. Some of the worst race riots in the history of the United States took place that summer. Racial unrest was seen in Boston;

Johnson with his daughter Luci at her wedding reception at the White House in 1966.

Buffalo; Toledo, Ohio; Grand Rapids, Michigan; and Newark, New Jersey. The deadliest riots took place in Detroit. In five days there, forty people died. Roughly two thousand were injured.[16]

Johnson was frustrated. He announced to the nation, "We will not tolerate lawlessness. We will not endure violence. It matters not by whom it is done or under what slogan or banner. . . . Pillage, looting, murder, and arson have nothing to do with civil rights. They are criminal conduct."[17]

Though Johnson spoke those strong words, he was nevertheless aware of the sorry living conditions of inner-city African Americans. He established a commission to look into the root causes of the riots and to offer solutions. Johnson wanted to show African Americans that he was trying to understand their problems. He also wished for whites to understand those concerns.[18]

The commission was called the National Advisory Commission on Civil Disorders. Heading it was Illinois Governor Otto Kerner. It became known as the Kerner Commission.

Johnson was right to be concerned about the reactions of white Americans. At first, many were sympathetic to the civil rights movement. But by now a large number of these same white people felt the movement had gotten out of hand. Martin Luther King, Jr.'s talk of brotherhood and nonviolence was becoming lost in the words of African-American militants.

Two of the more vocal militants were Stokely Carmichael and H. Rap Brown. They supported violence. They urged African Americans to get guns and take to the streets. To Carmichael, Brown, and other militants, white bigots were not the enemy—all whites were the enemy.

Carmichael said, "Our grandfathers and fathers had to run, run, run! My generation is out of breath! We just ain't running no more! And we ain't going to Vietnam! Do you dig what I'm saying, white pig? From now on, it's black power!"[19]

To law-abiding whites there was no excuse for these words and actions. Many craved a return to law and order. They had lost faith in the civil rights movement. This feeling became known as "white backlash."

At the same time, the war in Vietnam spurred many young white people to reject their parents' values. To them, their parents' rigid ways of thinking had brought on what they considered to be an unjust and unnecessary war. If that was the case, maybe their parents' other values were wrong, too. These young idealists believed people should spend more effort helping the poor and less for their own personal gains. They questioned the old order of priorities and beliefs. These were not simply rebellious teenagers. Many were college age or older.

In the 1940s and 1950s, a person who was aware of the latest trends and attitudes was called "hep." In the 1960s, the word became "hip." People who were "hip" became known as "hippies." Soon the term *hippie* was used to describe these rebellious young people.

In a way, they were rebelling in much the same manner that Johnson did when he was young. And just as Johnson had escaped to California, many hippies made California their unofficial capital. They flocked in great numbers to San Francisco.

While Johnson had rebelled in a less outwardly obvious way, hippies did so in their own manner. They made it a point to act and look as different as possible from the establishment (powerful people in business and government). They grew their hair long. They experimented with illegal drugs. They embraced rock music. Since flowers represented peace and beauty, some wore flowers in their hair. Men burned their draft cards (women are not subject to be drafted into the military). Many supported African-American militants. And they despised the war in Vietnam.

George Reedy recalled that Johnson was puzzled by the way America's young people turned against him. Reedy said, "He was bewildered by that. Johnson thought he had done more for young people than any other president."[20]

Not all war protesters were hippies. By now, senators, congresspeople, and Americans in all walks of life openly opposed the war. However, those who took part in active protests were mostly young. After all, they were the ones who would soon be drafted.

As they marched in protests, they chanted antiwar slogans. One was, "One, two, three, four. We don't want your rotten war." Others were personal attacks at Johnson, such as, "Hey, hey LBJ. How many boys did you kill today?"

An anthem of the antiwar advocates was a song by the rock band Country Joe and the Fish. The leader, Country Joe McDonald, was an army veteran turned antiwar hippie. The song was called, "I-Feel-Like-I'm-Fixin'-to-Die Rag."

This song condemned the war for having no purpose. The lyrics said that men being drafted to fight the war did not even know what they were risking their lives for. The song went on to blast the views of the United States military. According to the song, the military saw the North Vietnamese only as a mass of Communists rather than as individual people with families trying to unify their homeland.

One entire verse of the song criticized American companies that manufactured weapons. It said these companies did not care how many people died as long as they could make incredible amounts of money selling their weapons.[21]

In addition, "I-Feel-Like-I'm-Fixin'-to-Die Rag" sported a very strong "in your face" attitude. Country Joe and the Fish were not politely disagreeing with President Johnson and the military. They were symbolically spitting in the faces of their nation's leaders.

However, there were still many Americans who supported the war. Included were veterans who had fought in World War II. These people were sickened by such songs. They saw hippies and antiwar protesters as

Many antiwar protesters blamed Johnson for the escalation of violence in Vietnam. The protesters pictured marched on the Pentagon on October 21, 1967.

unpatriotic. A large number viewed the protesters as spoiled kids who were a disgrace to their country. Those who burned their draft cards were seen as traitors. The prowar movement summed up their views with the slogan: "America. Love it or leave it."

At times the two groups clashed in the streets. Often, violence broke out and injuries were a result. Between the war protests and race riots, it appeared as if Johnson had lost control of the nation.

His dream of the Great Society had all but vanished. Some say that Johnson once believed that if he withdrew from Vietnam, he would lose the respect of Congress and not get his Great Society programs passed. As it turned out, staying in Vietnam was what killed his Great Society.

On November 29, 1967, Johnson received the news that his secretary of defense, Robert McNamara, was quitting. McNamara had been behind the war since the Kennedy days. Many considered him the main architect of the war.

To this day, many believe McNamara's decision shocked Johnson. Johnson's press secretary, George Christian, disagrees. He said McNamara and Johnson had had a falling-out. Christian noted, "Johnson thought it was time for McNamara to leave. It was a mutual consent. McNamara did not just walk in and quit. Johnson played a big role in McNamara's departure."[22]

The Johnsons had a break from the gloominess of politics on December 9. They celebrated a second

In 1967, Johnson holds a press conference in the Oval Office. Most of the questions being asked related to the Vietnam War.

wedding, as daughter Lynda was married in the White House to a marine named Charles Robb.

At the end of the month, Johnson took a trip to Vietnam to visit the troops firsthand. He emphasized his support for both the fighting men and the war.

What many consider the turning point of the war came in January 1968. Tet is the name of a holiday celebrating the Vietnamese new year. During Tet 1968, the Communists began a series of major offensive attacks throughout South Vietnam. They hoped to start an uprising of the South Vietnamese people against their own government and the Americans.

The Tet Offensive lasted two months. It failed in its

objective to spark an uprising. However, the Communists proved they meant business. Even Americans who supported the war realized it would not end soon.

Walter Cronkite was a newscaster for CBS television. Some called him the most trusted man in America. With his gray hair and dignified manner, Cronkite was a father figure to millions. After the Tet Offensive began, Cronkite produced and hosted a documentary on the status of the war. It aired on February 27, 1968.

Cronkite ended the broadcast with something unusual for television. He gave his own personal view of the nation's prospects in the war. He stated that the war could not be won. He said:

> For it seems now more certain than ever that the bloody experience of Vietnam is to end in a stalemate. . . . But it is increasingly clear to this reporter that the only rational way out then will be to negotiate, not as victims but as an honorable people who lived up to their pledge to defend democracy and did the best they could.[23]

It was then that Johnson told George Christian words that have become famous. Christian remembered, "He turned to me and said, 'If I've lost Cronkite, I've lost the country.'"[24]

Christian explained, "I was a little surprised he'd say it [his reaction] that strongly, but sometimes he was a moody person. He knew Cronkite had such great credibility."[25]

Christian clarified the situation. "It wasn't that the country suddenly went against Johnson's war policies or

SOURCE DOCUMENT

THE SECRETARY OF DEFENSE
WASHINGTON

February 23, 1968

Dear Mr. President

I cannot find words to express to you the feelings that lie in my heart.

Fifty-one months ago you asked me to serve in your cabinet. No other period in my life has brought so much struggle -- or so much satisfaction. The struggle would have been infinitely greater and the satisfaction immeasurably less if I had not received your full support every step of the way.

No man could fail to be proud of service in an administration which has recorded the progress yours has in the fields of civil rights, health, and education. One hundred years of neglect can not be overcome overnight. But you have pushed, dragged, and cajoled the nation into basic reforms from which my children and my childrens' children will benefit for decades to come. I know the price you have paid, both personally and politically. Every citizen of our land is in your debt.

I will not say goodbye -- you know you have but to call and I will respond.

Sincerely

Bob

This letter from Robert McNamara praises the president. It was written after McNamara quit his post as secretary of defense, a decision influenced by Johnson.

against the war. When Johnson made that statement he meant, 'We're slipping.' He saw it as a watershed [a critical point]. . . ."[26]

A presidential election was to be held that year. With over five hundred thousand American troops fighting in Vietnam, the war was the major issue.[27] The nation's first primary election takes place in New Hampshire. In 1968, Minnesota senator Eugene McCarthy ran against Johnson as a peace candidate.

Johnson won the Democratic primary. However, McCarthy won a startling 42 percent of the vote.[28] It showed the public's lack of confidence in Johnson's leadership.

Then on March 16, Senator Robert Kennedy

In 1967 Johnson visits wounded soldiers at Cam Rahn Bay hospital in South Vietnam.

announced he would run against Johnson for the Democratic nomination. Kennedy was the brother of President John F. Kennedy.

Johnson gave a speech on March 31 that is now legendary. He ordered a stop to the bombing of North Vietnam. Then he dropped a verbal bombshell. He announced, "I shall not seek, and I will not accept the nomination of my party for another term as your President."[29]

To Americans, it seemed that Johnson had had enough. What Americans did not know is that Johnson had made his decision not to run months earlier. George Christian said, "He started talking to me about it [not running] in 1967. He was concerned about his health, about maybe having a stroke. He didn't want to be like Woodrow Wilson, not really being President in his last few years. After the New Hampshire primary, [it] was a convenient time to make the announcement. But he had decided not to run months before."[30]

(President Woodrow Wilson suffered a stroke and spent his last year and a half in office as a weak and feeble man. Some historians say because of Wilson's poor health, he was physically unable to fulfill his duties as president.)

Since Johnson would not be president again, he lacked real power at the end of his term. An officeholder in his position is called a "lame duck." Johnson was a lame duck for the next nine and a half months. But what a shocking time it was!

Finally, my fellow Americans, let me say this.

Of those to whom much is given, much is asked. I cannot say -- no man could say -- that no more will be asked of us. Yet I believe that now -- no less than when the decade began -- this generation of Americans is willing to --

> "pay any price, bear any burden, meet any hardship,
> support any friend, oppose any foe, to assure the
> survival and the success of liberty."

Since those words were spoken by John F. Kennedy, the people of America have kept that compact with mankind's noblest cause. We shall continue to keep it.

Yet I believe we must always be mindful of this one thing:

Whatever the trials and tests ahead, the ultimate strength of our country and our cause will lie not in powerful weapons or infinite resources or boundless wealth -- but in the unity of our people.

This I believe very deeply.

Throughout my public career, I have followed the personal philosophy that I am a free man, an American, a public servant, and a member of my party -- in that order, always and only. For

In this excerpt of an address given to the nation on March 31, 1968, Johnson offers a word of advice to Americans before announcing that he will not seek a second term of the presidency.

Three days after Johnson's speech was delivered, Ho Chi Minh said he would agree to peace negotiations. It would be a long time before they took place.

Four days after Johnson's speech, Martin Luther King, Jr., was shot and killed in Memphis. In response, riots erupted in America's inner cities. A drifter and petty criminal named James Earl Ray later pleaded guilty to the crime. Two months later, Robert Kennedy was assassinated in Los Angeles by an Arab immigrant named Sirhan B. Sirhan.

The Democratic National Convention took place in late August in Chicago. Vice-President Hubert Humphrey received the presidential nomination.

Johnson (lying in front, left) lounges with friends on the grounds of his Texas ranch toward the end of his presidency.

Outside the convention hall, police and antiwar demonstrators battled each other in the streets of Chicago. The Democratic party was sorely divided. Republican nominee Richard Nixon promised a return to law and order. To many Americans, it was about time.

Richard Nixon was elected president on November 5, 1968. On January 20, 1969, Nixon took the oath of office. Lyndon Johnson was again a private citizen.

8

THE QUIET
YEARS

L yndon and Lady Bird Johnson flew back to Texas
the afternoon of January 20, 1969. Their plane
landed at an air base instead of a public airport.
It was feared there would be masses of antiwar
protesters at a public airport.

Johnson was happy to be out of the White House.[1]

Still, it was a shock returning to private life. When
the Johnsons returned to their ranch, they found their
luggage in a big pile. Johnson wrote, "For the first time
in five years there were no aides to carry the bags
inside."[2]

Lady Bird laughed and compared their lives to
Cinderella's. She said, "The coach has turned back into
a pumpkin, and the mice have all run away."[3]

At first, retirement was hard for the former

president.[4] He was used to being busy. So he took an active role in running his ranch. In a way he ran it in the same manner that he had run his office as president. Before, he held morning meetings with his advisors. Now, he met in the morning with ranch workers. He told them what goals needed to be reached on the ranch. Tractors had to be fixed. Steers needed tending to.

Like many retired presidents, Johnson decided to write his memoirs. Instead of discussing his entire life however, Johnson chose to cover only the years of his presidency.

Johnson had more fun taking tourists around the replica of his birthplace. The reconstructed birthplace was transferred to the National Park Service in 1970. It became one part of the Lyndon B. Johnson National Historical Park. After his memoirs were published in 1971, Johnson often autographed copies for tourists visiting the site.

A staff member named Yolanda Boozer said, "He would stop at the birthplace himself and shake hands with people and say, 'Aren't ya gonna buy one of my books?'. . . 'Now if you do I'll sign it right here—give me a pen!' And he'd start signing—and before we knew it there was a crowd and a line of people."[5]

In 1971, his presidential library opened on the campus of the University of Texas in Austin on May 22. More than three thousand guests came to the event.[6] President Richard Nixon, former Vice-President Hubert

Humphrey, and Barry Goldwater all attended. It was a huge party featuring a giant Texas-sized barbecue serving pork ribs, beef brisket, and chicken.

Johnson looked out at the gathering and said,

> On behalf of Lady Bird and myself, I want to tell you how much joy you give us for your presence here today. I look out into that sea of faces, and I see men that I have engaged with debate through the years—men and women who have followed us every mile of the long road. And it gives me nothing but the greatest satisfaction—one of the greatest of my life. Thank you very much.[7]

The day was not all joy. Protesters shouting antiwar slogans were also on hand.

The east bedroom of Johnson's birthplace in Stonewall, Texas.

The Lyndon B. Johnson Presidential Library opened May 22, 1971, on the campus of the University of Texas in Austin.

Public appearances like that were rare for Lyndon Johnson. Some retired presidents make a second career out of teaching and giving lectures. Johnson was happy to stay at his ranch.

Yolanda Boozer remembered, "He really loved the Ranch and that was the reason he didn't want to accept any invitations to go anywhere. He just didn't want to leave."[8]

Perhaps Johnson knew his life was ending and wanted to spend his last days on the land he loved. He had stopped taking care of himself, just as he did following his heart attack in 1955. He began smoking cigarettes. He was also drinking alcohol more heavily than before.

Johnson's appearance changed, too. Because of the hippies' influence, men across the country were wearing their hair longer. Johnson, too, wore his hair longer. His gray hair curled in thick ringlets at the back of his head.

A Johnson biographer named Ronnie Dugger said he felt Johnson was trying to look like a hippie. Dugger said, "He looked like he was identifying with the kids who had been demonstrating against the war. Maybe he was trying to say to them, 'Hey, I understand. If I had been young, I might have done the same thing.'"[9]

At the LBJ Library and Museum, numerous archive boxes are stored above a mural of Johnson and the presidents he admired.

During his retirement, LBJ grew his hair long, perhaps as an effort to relate to the young people who opposed the war in Vietnam.

The United States' role in Vietnam was winding down. President Nixon gradually withdrew American troops. By 1972, only twenty-five thousand remained.[10] Most were not fighting men but military advisors. Still, some Americans thought Nixon should have ended all American involvement in Vietnam years earlier. They thought the war was still dragging on too long.

One of these men was South Dakota senator George McGovern. The Democrats chose him as their party's candidate for president in 1972.

In most cases, former presidents are invited to speak at their parties' political conventions. The year 1972 was not like most cases. Johnson was still unpopular. Some might have said he was a disgraced former president. There was also fear that Johnson's appearance might lead to a repeat of the 1968 Chicago convention riots. Johnson was not invited to the 1972 Democratic National Convention.

Most Americans believed McGovern's ideas were too liberal. Richard M. Nixon was reelected in a huge landslide, winning in forty-nine states. McGovern won only Massachusetts.

As the year 1972 came to a close, Johnson's health was failing. He suffered from a heart condition called angina, in which not enough blood flows to one's heart. It often causes severe chest pains.

On the afternoon of January 22, 1973, Lyndon Johnson died of a heart attack at his ranch. He was buried in the family cemetery along the banks of the Pedernales River. It was not far from where he used to play as a child.

Just five days after Johnson died, the United States and North Vietnam signed a peace treaty. The United States would withdraw all remaining troops. North Vietnam would release all United States prisoners of war. A cease-fire was declared.

North Vietnam and South Vietnam continued fighting until January 1975. The South Vietnamese government finally collapsed. North Vietnam had won the war.

9

LEGACY

Lady Bird Johnson still lives quietly at the LBJ Ranch. She has continued in her efforts toward making America more beautiful. In 1995 she founded the National Wildflower Research Center in Austin.

Daughter Luci, Johnson's first to be married, dropped out of college when her husband went to serve in Vietnam.

She and Patrick Nugent had four children before they divorced in 1979. Luci then married a Scottish-born banker named Ian Turpin in 1984. The Turpins live in Austin where they manage the family business, which includes three radio stations. In 1997 Luci finished college. At age forty-nine she earned a degree from tiny St. Edward's University in Austin.

Luci said at the time, "I didn't want to be the first female in four generations [in my family] not to have a university degree."[1]

Lynda and Charles Robb had three daughters. She became first lady of Virginia when Charles was elected governor of Virginia in 1981. He was later elected a United States senator from Virginia.

Lyndon Johnson's memory has been honored in several ways. In 1973 the Texas state legislature passed a law that made Johnson's birthday a state holiday. It is celebrated every August 27 in Texas. Also in 1973, the National Aeronautics and Space Administration (NASA) headquarters in Houston was officially named the Lyndon B. Johnson Space Center.

But how do people judge him as a president?

Many give Lyndon Johnson poor marks as president. They say he led his nation into a failed war. They add that he was not honest with the American people regarding his country's performance in that war. Many Americans who supported the war in its time now concede it was wrong for the United States to become so deeply involved in it. One is Robert McNamara, the very man who, as secretary of defense, helped map out the war for seven years.

In 1995 McNamara wrote about those who supported the war: "We were wrong, terribly wrong."[2] Those words shocked many Americans, especially Vietnam veterans.

Others criticize Johnson for his Great Society

programs. Since the early 1980s, there has been a movement away from big government programs such as the Great Society. In 1980 conservative Republican Ronald Reagan was elected president. Reagan believed many ideas opposite to Johnson's. He said that government programs make people dependent. He felt that people will not work as hard if they rely on government programs to bail them out of trouble. To help the needy, Reagan supported private charities.

Under Reagan's leadership, some government programs were cut. After Reagan left office in 1989, his policies of smaller government were continued by the next two presidents: conservative Republican George Bush (1989–1993) and moderate Democrat Bill Clinton (1993–present).

There was an even greater turn away from the policy of big government in 1994. There was no presidential election that year, but the Republican party took control of both the Senate and House of Representatives. Georgia congressman Newt Gingrich was chosen speaker of the House. He condemned Johnson's programs.

In 1995 Gingrich said, "It is impossible to take the Great Society structure of bureaucracy and have any hope of fixing it. They [Great Society programs] are a disaster."[3]

President Clinton saw the 1994 vote as a mandate for smaller government. He claimed that the era of big government was over.

Yet experts rank Lyndon Johnson highly as a president. A survey of over seven hundred historians was published in 1997. The survey ranked the forty-one presidents by their degrees of greatness. Lyndon Johnson finished twelfth.[4]

A similar survey of over eight hundred historians was conducted in 1982. In that survey Johnson ranked tenth.[5] That same year a survey of forty-nine of the nation's "leading historians and scholars" was conducted by the *Chicago Tribune*.[6] In that survey Johnson ranked twelfth.[7] How can that be? Certainly, Johnson gets high marks for his action on civil rights. Even those who opposed integration at the time agree today that the Civil Rights Act of 1964 and the Voting Rights Act of 1965 were the morally right things to do.

In spite of their votes in 1994, Americans may not have been saying the Great Society was a mistake. Johnson's former press secretary George Reedy said, "The amount of noise being made isn't necessarily what people are interested in. The press and the politicians might make a lot of noise, but it may not be what the people really care about."[8]

George Christian explained, "Johnson was president at a time of national need for action in a lot of areas, things like Medicare, the civil rights act, aid to education, brand-new concepts like Head Start and the Job Corps. He tried to uplift people who couldn't look after themselves. Now we feel government has done all it needs to do."[9]

Christian continued, "Some criticism of the Great Society is valid. If Johnson were alive today, he'd have some criticisms of some programs. No question in the case of welfare, we've created a permanent welfare class. But Johnson didn't create that. Public assistance had been around for a long time before Johnson [was president].

"Johnson didn't like wasteful spending. People forget that he submitted that last balanced budget that we've had."[10]

Reedy and Christian might have valid points. Once the Republican-controlled Congress of the mid-1990s actually tried to cut government programs, it ran into problems. It seems that although many Americans claim they want small government, just as many do not want to cut Medicare. Many do not want to cut funding for public television or the national parks.

On the other hand, conservative Republicans did not want to cut the defense budget. It seems as if Americans say they want to cut government programs—but they really want to cut only those that do not benefit them personally.

However, the Vietnam War still haunts the nation. Politicians in the 1990s who avoided the draft in the 1960s were condemned by veterans' groups. These include President Clinton and George Bush's vice-president, Dan Quayle. Some extremists have claimed that President Johnson had truly evil plans concerning the war.

Just after the Warren Commission Report was released, most Americans accepted it as fact. That is no longer the case. Hundreds of books have been written claiming the Warren Commission Report was wrong. These books say either that Oswald did not act alone or that he did not even shoot Kennedy. The most extreme views say that government agencies such as the Central Intelligence Agency (CIA) or Federal Bureau of Investigation (FBI) were behind Kennedy's murder.

Perhaps the most famous theory was expressed in a major movie called *JFK*. It came out in 1991 and was written and directed by Oliver Stone. In the movie, Stone suggests that President Johnson was behind the death of President Kennedy. Stone concludes that Kennedy wanted to end the United States' involvement in Vietnam. He says Kennedy was killed so that Johnson, the military, and businesses that supply weapons to the military could profit from the war.

The majority of journalists and historians strongly disagree. Veteran journalist Walter Cronkite said, "This Oliver Stone junk—absolute junk that that guy perpetrated on an unsuspecting generation—planted thoughts about Lyndon Johnson himself plotting the assassination. Furthermore, if there had been the kind of conspiracy that that movie made out—or any of these major conspiracy theorists . . . I don't believe for one minute it could have been kept a secret for all these years."[11]

Despite all the conspiracy theories, the Warren Commission Report has never been proven wrong.[12]

There was one other commission Johnson established: the Kerner Commission. In 1968 the Kerner Commission report was released. It said, "This is our basic conclusion: our nation is moving toward two societies, one black, one white—separate and unequal."[13] Many today agree that the Kerner Commission conclusion was right on target.

So what is Johnson's legacy? Was he a liar or a goodhearted leader who wanted the best for his people? Did he recklessly lead the nation into a failed war, or was he merely a victim of trying to follow the policies that the majority of Americans felt were right? Was he a brilliant politician or a shifty wheeler-dealer?

Conservative Republicans tend to believe the worst about Lyndon Johnson. Many other Americans feel he accomplished a great deal in his administration. In the opinion of most historians, however, Lyndon Baines Johnson will clearly be ranked in the top quarter of their lists.

Chronology

1908—Born in Stonewall, Texas, on August 27 to Rebekah Baines and Sam Ealy Johnson, Jr.

1913—Family moves to Johnson City, Texas.

1924—Graduates high school; moves to California.

1925—Returns home from California.

1927—Enrolls at Southwest Texas State Teachers College.

1928—Earns two-year college degree early.

1928–1929—Teaches school in Cotulla, Texas.

1929—Returns to Southwest Texas State Teachers College as student.

1930—Earns bachelor's degree; teaches school in Pearsall, Texas.

1930–1931—Teaches school in Houston, Texas.

1931–1935—Works for Congressman Richard Kleberg in Washington, D.C.

1934—Marries Claudia Alta "Lady Bird" Taylor.

1935–1937—Works for National Youth Administration, part of Franklin D. Roosevelt's New Deal.

1937—Elected to House of Representatives.

1941—Loses election for United States Senate.

1942—Serves in World War II.

1944—Daughter Lynda Bird born.

1947—Daughter Lucy (Luci) Baines born.

1948—Elected to United States Senate.

1951—Named Democratic party whip; buys LBJ Ranch.

1954—Reelected to United States Senate.

1955—Named Senate majority leader; suffers heart attack.

1957—Helps arrange compromise Civil Rights Act of 1957.

1960—Wins election as vice-president under John F. Kennedy.

1961—Vice-president of the United States.
–1963

1963—Becomes president of the United States after death of President Kennedy in November; names Warren Commission to investigate Kennedy assassination.

1964—Declares War on Poverty; Civil Rights Act of 1964 passed.

Tonkin Gulf Resolution passed.

Elected as president in his own right.

1965—Sends first United States combat troops to Vietnam.

Passes many Great Society programs, including Medicare.

Sends Marines to Dominican Republic.

Signs Voting Rights Act of 1965.

Watts riots.

1966—"Credibility gap."

Large-scale race riots in several cities.

Continues sending troops to Vietnam.

1967—Widens Vietnam War.

Massive race riots.

Establishes Kerner Commission.

Visits Vietnam in December.

1968—After Tet Offensive in Vietnam, announces he will not run for another term as president.

Stops bombing of North Vietnam.

Martin Luther King, Jr., and Robert F. Kennedy assassinated.

Antiwar protesters and police clash at Democratic National Convention.

1969—Leaves presidency on January 20; retires to LBJ Ranch in Texas.

1971—Lyndon B. Johnson Presidential Library opens.

1973—Dies of a heart attack on January 22.

Chapter Notes

Chapter 1. A Long Time Coming

1. Personal interview with George Christian, November 13, 1997.

2. *American Experience*, "LBJ, Part 2," KERA Productions in association with David Grubin Productions, Inc., executive producer Judy Crichton, 1991.

3. *History Undercover*, "The Johnson Tapes," Channel Four Television Corporation, executive producer George Carey, 1997.

4. Merle Miller, *Lyndon: An Oral Biography* (New York: G.P. Putnam's Sons, 1980), p. 371.

5. Irving Bernstein, *Guns or Butter: The Presidency of Lyndon Johnson* (New York: Oxford University Press, 1996), p. 79.

Chapter 2. "Such a Friendly Baby"

1. Ronnie Dugger, *The Politician: The Life and Times of Lyndon Johnson* (New York: W.W. Norton & Company, 1982), p. 65.

2. Merle Miller, *Lyndon: An Oral Biography* (New York: G.P. Putnam's Sons, 1980), p. 7.

3. Robert Dallek, *Lone Star Rising* (New York: Oxford University Press, Inc., 1991), p. 32.

4. Miller, p. 8.

5. National Park Service, transcript of audio tour, Lyndon B. Johnson National Historical Park, revised March 15, 1973.

6. *Biography* television series, "Lyndon Johnson" episode, ABC News Productions in association with and Arts and Entertainment Network, executive producer Lisa Zeff, 1996.

7. Ibid.

8. Doris Kearns, *Lyndon Johnson & the American Dream* (New York: Signet Books, 1976), p. 27.

9. Dallek, p. 44.

10. Kearns, p. 39.

11. *Biography* television series.

Chapter 3. "I Never Had a Chance, But You Do"

1. Merle Miller, *Lyndon: An Oral Biography* (New York: G.P. Putnam's Sons, 1980), p. 28.

2. Ibid.

3. Robert Dallek, *Lone Star Rising* (New York: Oxford University Press, Inc., 1991), p. 66.

4. Ronnie Dugger, *The Politician: The Life and Times of Lyndon Johnson* (New York: W.W. Norton & Company, 1982), p. 110.

5. Ibid., p. 111.

6. Doris Kearns, *Lyndon Johnson & the American Dream* (New York: Signet Books, 1976), pp. 59–60.

7. Dallek, p. 78.

8. Clarke Newlon, *LBJ: The Man from Johnson City* (New York: Dodd, Mead & Company, 1964), p. 37.

9. Dallek, p. 80.

10. Miller, p. 32.

11. Dallek, p. 90.

Chapter 4. Landslide Lyndon?

1. Robert Dallek, *Lone Star Rising* (New York: Oxford University Press, Inc., 1991), p. 101.

2. Paul F. Boller, Jr., *Presidential Wives* (New York: Oxford University Press, 1988), p. 380.

3. *Biography*, television series, "Lyndon Johnson" episode, ABC News Productions in association with and Arts and Entertainment Network, executive producer Lisa Zeff, 1996.

4. Boller, p. 381.

5. Sam Houston Johnson, *My Brother Lyndon* (New York: Cowles Book Company, Inc., 1970), p. 51.

6. Ibid.

7. Ibid.

8. Richard Harwood and Haynes Johnson, *Lyndon* (New York: Praeger Publishers, 1973), p. 31.

9. Dallek, p. 161.

10. *American Experience*, "LBJ, Part 1," KERA Productions in association with David Grubin Productions, Inc., executive producer Judy Crichton, 1991.

11. Ibid.

12. Ibid.

13. Dallek, p. 209.

14. Ibid. p. 220.

15. Robert Caro, *The Years of Lyndon Johnson: The Path to Power* (New York: Alfred A. Knopf, 1982), p. 733.

16. Merle Miller, *Lyndon: An Oral Biography* (New York: G.P. Putnam's Sons, 1980), p. 88.

17. Miller, p. 118.

18. David C. Whitney, *The American Presidents* (Garden City, N.Y.: Doubleday & Co., Inc., 1978), p. 337.

19. National Park Service, transcript of audio tour, Lyndon B. Johnson National Historical Park, revised March 15, 1973.

20. William A. DeGregorio, *The Complete Book of U.S. Presidents* (New York: Wings Books, 1991), p. 568.

21. *Biography* television series.

22. DeGregorio, p. 568.

23. Miller, p. 212.

Chapter 5. Into the Oval Office

1. Transcript from LBJ Library, interview with Jack Valenti by T.H. Baker, June 14, 1969, tape 1, pp. 9–10.

2. Ibid., pp. 10–11.

3. Doris Kearns, *Lyndon Johnson & the American Dream* (New York: Signet Books, 1976), pp. 171–173.

4. Sam Houston Johnson, *My Brother Lyndon* (New York: Cowles Book Company, Inc., 1970), p. 108.

5. Ibid. p. 112.

6. *Biography*, television series, "Lyndon Johnson" episode, ABC News Productions in association with and Arts and Entertainment Network, executive producer Lisa Zeff, 1996.

7. William A. DeGregorio, *The Complete Book of U.S. Presidents* (New York: Wings Books, 1991), p. 556.

8. Ibid.

9. *The Dallas Morning News, November 22: The Day Remembered*, (Dallas: Taylor Publishing Company, 1990), p. 42.

10. Ibid.

11. Ibid., p. 48.

12. *History Undercover*, "The Johnson Tapes," Channel Four Television Corporation, executive producer George Carey, 1997.

13. Ibid.

14. Lyndon Baines Johnson, *The Choices We Face* (New York: Bantam Books, 1969), p. 73.

15. *American Experience,* "LBJ, Part 1," KERA Productions in association with David Grubin Productions, Inc., executive producer Judy Crichton, 1991.

16. Irving Bernstein, *Guns or Butter: The Presidency of Lyndon Johnson* (New York: Oxford University Press, 1996), p. 338.

17. Robert S. McNamara, *In Retrospect: The Tragedy and Lessons of Vietnam* (New York: Random House, 1995), p. 128.

18. *American Experience,* "LBJ, Part 2," KERA Productions in association with David Grubin Productions, Inc., executive producer Judy Crichton, 1991.

Chapter 6. One Remarkable Year

1. John Steinbeck, "A President—Not a Candidate," 1964 Democratic National Convention program book, (Washington, D.C.: Democratic Convention Program Book Committee, 1964), pp. 94–95.

2. Paul F. Boller, Jr., *Presidential Campaigns* (New York: Oxford University Press, 1985), p. 310.

3. Ibid., p. 311.

4. Ibid.

5. William A. DeGregorio, *The Complete Book of U.S. Presidents* (New York: Wings Books, 1991), p. 571.

6. *The World Almanac and Book of Facts* (Mahwah, N.J.: World Almanac Books, 1997), p. 425.

7. Ibid.

8. Doris Kearns, *Lyndon Johnson & the American Dream* (New York: Signet Books, 1976), p. 219.

9. Robert S. McNamara, *In Retrospect: The Tragedy and Lessons of Vietnam* (New York: Times Books, 1995), pp. 167–168.

10. Lyndon Baines Johnson, *The Vantage Point* (New York: Holt, Rinehart and Winston, 1971), p. 128.

11. "The Class of the Twentieth Century," television program, years 1963–1968, CEL Communications, Inc. and Arts and Entertainment Network, 1991.

12. Clifton Daniel, editor in chief, *Chronicle of the 20th Century* (Liberty, Mo.: JL International Publishing, 1992), p. 931.

13. Ibid., p. 933.

14. Johnson, p. 191.

15. McNamara, p. 169.

16. Daniel, p. 936.

17. David McCullough, *Truman* (New York: Simon & Schuster, 1992), p. 984.

18. Johnson, p. 166.

19. Personal interview with George Christian, November 13, 1997.

20. Irving Bernstein, *Guns or Butter: The Presidency of Lyndon Johnson* (New York: Oxford University Press, 1996), p. 387.

21. Personal interview with George Reedy, October 8, 1997.

22. *American Experience*, "LBJ, Part 3," KERA Productions in association with David Grubin Productions, Inc., executive producer Judy Crichton, 1991.

23. Ibid.

Chapter 7. Johnson's War

1. Personal interview with George Christian, November 13, 1997.

2. *Year by Year*, "1966," History Channel, Producer David Rein, 1996.

3. Robert S. McNamara, *In Retrospect: The Tragedy and Lessons of Vietnam* (New York: Times Books, 1995), p. 33.

4. Richard Harwood and Haynes Johnson, *Lyndon* (New York: Praeger Publishers, 1973), p. 122.

5. Ibid.

6. Clifton Daniel, editor in chief, *Chronicle of the 20th Century* (Liberty, Mo.: JL International Publishing, 1992), p. 947.

7. David McCullough, *Truman* (New York: Simon & Schuster, 1992), p. 457.

8. *20/20* broadcast, ABC News, 1995.

9. Eric F. Goldman, *The Tragedy of Lyndon Johnson* (New York: Alfred A. Knopf, 1969), p. 410.

10. *American Experience*, "LBJ, Part 4," KERA Productions in association with David Grubin Productions, Inc., executive producer Judy Crichton, 1991.

11. Personal interview with George Reedy, October 8, 1997.

12. Ibid.

13. George Howe Colt and Doris G. Kinney, "White House Families," *Life*, November 1984, p. 42.

14. Lady Bird Johnson, *A White House Diary* (New York: Holt, Rinehart and Winston, 1970), p. 411.

15. Paul F. Boller, Jr., *Presidential Wives* (New York: Oxford University Press, 1988), p. 388.

16. Ibid., p. 419.

17. *American Experience*, "LBJ, Part 4."

18. Joseph A. Califano, Jr., *The Triumph & Tragedy of Lyndon Johnson: The White House Years* (New York: Simon & Schuster, 1991), p. 219.

19. Gordon Parks, "What Became of the Prophets of Rage?" *Life*, Spring 1988, p. 32.

20. Personal interview with George Reedy, October 8, 1997.

21. Correspondence from Tim Moore, Rock and Roll Hall of Fame, April 10, 1997.

22. Personal interview with George Christian, November 13, 1997.

23. *Cronkite Remembers*, A production of CBS News in association with Cronkite/Ward & Company, senior producer David Browning, 1996.

24. Personal interview with George Christian, November 13, 1997.

25. Ibid.

26. Ibid.

27. Ted Yanak and Pam Cornelison, *The Great American History Fact-Finder* (New York: Houghton Mifflin Company, 1993), p. 396.

28. Califano, p. 265.

29. "The Class of the Twentieth Century," television program, years 1963–1968, CEL Communications, Inc. and Arts and Entertainment Network, 1991.

30. Personal interview with George Christian, November 13, 1997.

Chapter 8. The Quiet Years

1. Lyndon Baines Johnson, *The Vantage Point* (New York: Holt, Rinehart and Winston, 1971), p. 566.

2. Ibid., p. 568.

3. Ibid.

4. Merle Miller, *Lyndon: An Oral Biography* (New York: G. P. Putnam's Sons, 1980), p. 543.

5. Ibid., p. 549.

6. Martin Waldron, "Nixon Hails Johnson Library at Dedication," *New York Times*, May 23, 1971, p. 1.

7. Transcript from LBJ Library, "Remarks of President Johnson at the LBJ Library Dedication," May 22, 1971, p. 4.

8. Miller, p. 546.

9. *American Experience*, "LBJ, Part 4," KERA Productions in association with David Grubin Productions, Inc., executive producer Judy Crichton, 1991.

10. William A. DeGregorio, *The Complete Book of U.S. Presidents* (New York: Wings Books, 1991), p. 595.

Chapter 9. Legacy

1. Andrea Stone, "President's Daughter Makes Up for Lost Time," *USA Today*, May 7, 1997, p. 4D.

2. Robert S. McNamara, *In Retrospect: The Tragedy and Lessons of Vietnam* (New York: Times Books, 1995), p. xvi.

3. *20/20* broadcast, ABC News, 1995.

4. William J. Ridings, Jr., and Stuart B. McIver, *Rating the Presidents: A Ranking of U.S. Leaders, From the Great and Honorable to the Dishonest and Incompetent* (Secaucus, N.J.: Citadel Press, 1997), p. xi.

5. Robert K. Murray and Tim H. Blessing, "The Presidential Performance Study: A Progress Report," *The Journal of American History*, December 1983, p. 540.

6. Ibid., p. 536.

7. Ibid., p. 540.

8. Personal interview with George Reedy, October 8, 1997.

9. Personal interview with George Christian, November 13, 1997.

10. Ibid.

11. *Cronkite Remembers*, a production of CBS News in association with Cronkite/Ward & Company, senior producer David Browning, 1996.

12. Exhibit marker on display in The Sixth Floor historic site, Dallas, Texas.

13. Rhoda Lois Blumberg, *Civil Rights: The 1960s Freedom Struggle* (Boston: Twayne Publishers, 1991), p. 168.

Further Reading

Healey, Tim. *The 1960's*. New York: Franklin Watts, 1988.

Kent, Deborah. *The Vietnam War: "What Are We Fighting For?"* Springfield, N.J.: Enslow Publishers, 1994.

Myers, Walter Dean. *A Place Called Heartbreak: A Story of Vietnam*. Austin, Texas: Raintree Steck-Vaughn Publishers, 1993.

Pimlott, Dr. John. *Conflict in the 20th Century: The Cold War*. New York: Franklin Watts, 1987.

Stein, R. Conrad. *America the Beautiful: Texas*. Chicago: Children's Press, 1989.

Steins, Richard. *The Postwar Years: The Cold War and the Atomic Age (1950–1959)*. New York: Twenty-First Century Books, 1993.

Wills, Charles. *The Tet Offensive*. Morristown, N.J.: Silver Burdett Press, 1989.

Places to Visit

California

Richard Nixon Library and Birthplace, Yorba Linda. (714) 993-5075. Richard Nixon's presidential library has exhibits relating to the Vietnam War. Open year-round.

Connecticut

Museum of American Political Life, West Hartford. (860) 768-4090. The history of every U.S. presidential campaign is told through buttons, banners, photos, and videotape. Open year-round.

Massachusetts

The Museum at the John Fitzgerald Kennedy Library, Boston. (617) 929-4523. Kennedy's library has exhibits on the 1960 election and Johnson's years as vice-president. Open year-round.

Tennessee

The National Civil Rights Museum, Memphis. (901) 521-9699. The motel where Martin Luther King, Jr., was assassinated has been converted into a major museum covering the civil rights movement. Open year-round.

Texas

Lyndon B. Johnson Library and Museum, Austin. (512) 916-5137. Johnson's presidential library tells his life story.

Included are his 1968 limousine and a reproduction of the White House Oval Office. Open year-round.

Lyndon B. Johnson National Historical Park, Stonewall and Johnson City. (210) 868-7128. One can visit the replica of Johnson's birthplace, the one-room schoolhouse he attended, his boyhood home in Johnson City, the ranch grounds, and the burial site. (The ranch home is closed to the public because Lady Bird still lives there.) Open year-round.

Lyndon B. Johnson State Historical Park, Stonewall. (210) 644-2252. Here are a pioneer homestead and a living history farm depicting the time of President Johnson's ancestors. Open year-round.

Washington, D.C.

The White House. (202) 456-7041. Several rooms are open to visitors on certain weekday mornings. You can get tickets when you arrive or in advance through your senator or congressperson. Open year-round.

Vietnam Veterans Memorial. (202) 485-9875. The names of all those who died in the war are inscribed on a black granite V-shaped wall. Nearby are realistic, life-sized statues of three anonymous servicemen and three anonymous servicewomen aiding a wounded soldier. Open year-round.

Internet Addresses

Information on all United States presidents

home page—http://sunsite.unc.edu/lia/president/

John F. Kennedy Library Foundation

home page—http://www.cs.umb.edu/jfklibrary/
index.htm

Lyndon B. Johnson Library and Museum

home page—http://www.lbjlib.utexas.edu/

**The National Park Service, including
Lyndon B. Johnson National Historical Park and
Vietnam Veterans Memorial**

home page—http://www.nps.gov

The Richard Nixon Library and Birthplace

home page—http://www.chapman.edu/nixon

The White House

home page—http://www.whitehouse.gov/WH/
Welcome.html

White House Historical Association

home page—http://www.whitehousehistory.org

Index